The Enlightened Society

Cover art by Jane A. Evans

The Enlightened Society

JOHN L. HILL

A Quest Book

This publication made possible with the assistance of the Kern Foundation

The Theosophical Publishing House
Wheaton, Ill. U.S.A.
Madras, India / London, England

A Quest original. First edition 1987

The Theosophical Publishing House
306 West Geneva Road
Wheaton, IL 60187

A publication of the Theosophical Publishing House, a department of the Theosophical Society in America.

Library of Congress Cataloging in Publication Data

Hill, John L. (John Lawrence), 1960-
The enlightened society.

(A Quest Book)
Bibliography: p.
Includes index.
1. Philosophy. 2. Psychology. 3. Civilization, Modern—1950- I. Title.
B72.H53 1987 116 86-40403
ISBN 0-8356-0615-5 (pbk.)

Printed in the United States of America

To my parents, Ronald and Vilma, for their love and support, and to Ana, my wife, for her continued inspiration.

About the Author

John Lawrence Hill received a B.A. in Communication Studies and Philosophy and an M.A. in Philosophy from Northern Illinois University, where he taught logic and contemporary moral issues in the Philosophy Department. He is presently attending Georgetown University in Washington, D.C., where he is working toward a simultaneous law degree and doctorate in Philosophy.

The author is on the staff of *The Georgetown Journal of Legal Ethics*, the only major law journal dedicated to the study of ethical issues in the legal profession. He also attends classes at the Kennedy Institute of Ethics, a leading institution in the study of legal and ethical issues in medicine and science. His goal is to combine law and philosophy in the study of bioethics, becoming involved in the legal and philosophical implications of genetic engineering, euthanasia, abortion, and eugenics.

Mr. Hill attempts to combine an academic inquiry into psycho-spiritual development with a personal investigation of meditation and its effects. *The Enlightened Society* is the product of this effort.

Contents

Acknowledgments

I wish to thank Dale Snauwaert and Ann Lee Fischer, who reviewed portions of this book while it was still in an inchoate form. I also wish to thank Debbie Mahaffey, who edited, typed, and retyped the manuscript, and who, as a good friend, always brought her warmth and support to this project. Thanks also to Bradley White, Ronald White, and particularly Karon White Gibson for her obstinate belief in this book. Thanks go to my wife, Ana Guedea, both for her criticism and inspiration and for the hours of typing which she selflessly invested in this project. Finally, I would like to thank Shirley Nicholson, editor of Quest books, for all of her time, effort, and consideration in editing and revising the manuscript.

Introduction

It happens most often, when it happens at all, late at night, just before Everyman silently drifts off to sleep, surrendering yet another day to Morpheus. It is in the boundless twilight between waking and sleep that the usual and interminable preoccupations that take the mind captive by day disappear. It is during this interlude that the more important thoughts come to light, when the mind sinks beneath its own eddies and surface rushes, inexorably swept by a powerful undercurrent and brought to the very ground of existence. It is at these times that Everyman becomes the Philosopher.

The questions of who we are most essentially, what is our greatest potential, and how can that potential be realized come to the fore at these moments of midnight contemplation. Whether the just-completed day has been meaningful and worthwhile, whether life in general has been so, and how the prospect for tomorrow appears are the most basic questions anyone can put to himself. It is also at these times, however, that modern man may feel failed by contemporary philosophy.

One hundred and fifty years ago Henry David Thoreau said: "There are nowadays, professors of philosophy but not philosophers. To be a philosopher is not merely to have subtle thoughts, not even to found a school, but so to love wisdom as to live according to its dictates, a life of simplicity, independence, magnanimity and trust."

With half-concealed smiles, many a modern philosopher would nod politely at such sentimentalism. As one hard-nosed technician asserted, "Philosophy is not going about a mountain in a white sheet." This attitude, characterized by a general distrust of anything meaningfully said about the human condition, is pervasive today in academic philosophy.

Twentieth-century philosophy is almost completely dominated by the two schools of analytic philosophy and continental philosophy. The first group is most prevalent in England and America, the second in France, Germany, and the other countries of Europe. I do not believe it is too great a generalization to say that most Anglo-American analytic philosophers tend to look down on continental philosophers, who are influenced by existentialism and phenomenology, as imprecise, metaphysical obscurantists, while the continentals look upon the analytic thinkers as technicians who have lost touch with the fundamental issues. In America "hard" analytic philosophy has increasingly come under the criticism, partially justified, that it has retreated into an endless semantic merry-go-round. The definition and redefinition of precise concepts are cause for great controversy, while philosophy seems to have relinquished all hope of ascertaining what these terms mean in the human context.

Even more justified is the claim that philosophy has become self-absorbed with the process of its own methodology. Logical method, formerly the *means* to the answer of important questions, has now become the *subject* of a greater portion of study and debate in the discipline. Just as the bewildered neurotic gives up the outside world to wander about in the world of his own feelings and motivations, so the modern philosopher, equally bewildered with a world seemingly beyond human understanding, has traded questions of content for those of form, surrendering the realm of "why" for the less significant world of self-definition. It seems that analysis as a method has led to a distressing abnegation of the bigger issues. Where can modern man turn for answers at his midnight moments of contemplation?

Modern psychology, the other discipline that will be explored in the pages that follow, offers little more. As with philosophy, twentieth-century psychology has surrendered the area of greatest importance as "unscientific." Today, behavioristic psychology still dominates academic psychology in Europe and America. Behaviorism, of course, is the doctrine that holds that inner states of psychic being—subjective thoughts, motivation, and desires—are unimportant in the study of the individual. Because only external behavior can be objectively quantified, subjective mental processes are regarded as nothing more than a reification of outward physical activity. It is more than ironic that perhaps the most important school of psychology—supposedly the study of the mind—denies the very existence of the mind as a naive metaphysical construct for behavioral states and dispositions. For the behaviorist, the individual is simply an amalgam of reflex behaviors, learned behaviors, and dispositions to learned and reflex behavior. In essence, modern behaviorism has truly given up the study of causes for the cataloging of effects.

There are, of course, bright spots to be explored in both modern philosophy and psychology. In philosophy increasing numbers are searching for new directions in response to the current malaise. In psychology the advent of the "third force," psychoanalysis and behaviorism constituting the first and second, has brought humanistic and client-centered systems to popularity, and the transpersonal psychology movement addresses issues beyond the personal self. These approaches have always been greeted with more sympathy in the clinical setting, where the practitioner is faced with human reality rather than academic requirements of theoretical parsimony.

Despite these hopeful developments, which may constitute an important trend in the humanities and social sciences, what is most regrettable is that these fields have, to a great extent, left the world of human affairs. People in the real world, concerned with the problems of achieving self-identity and a meaningful life, are now more than ever before in desperate need of the guidance of these disciplines. But the philosopher has become logician, wizard of the alchemy of the a priori, while the contemporary academic psychologist has become the "rat pusher" and the "number cruncher," more at home with statistical arrays than with the confession of the alienated personality. As a society, even at the level of our most esteemed academic institutions, we seem to have developed a surplus of facts and a shortage of truth. The modern philosopher or psychologist is, more often than not, a man of limited horizons, a theorist without a vision. But what has become of the sage, the man who wears his truth out in the open, unceremoniously displaying it for all who care to notice? Could it be that our truths have gotten too thin to wear?

In this work I attempt to reconcile Western naturalism with an evolutionary and transcendent view of mankind. I embrace naturalism, but I reject reductionism. Body and mind are not two different substances, as some traditional religions contend. Further, they are not strictly identical, as modern reductionistic materialism holds. Rather, the human system is a hierarchical lattice of evolutionary development. This theory has been called "emergent evolutionism." The ethic I will put forward is humanistic, but it is not man as he now is who is the measure of all things. Rather, it is man as he *may be* that constitutes the ideal. Thus, my view of the human condition might be called "transcendent humanism." Finally, my use of the term "state of consciousness" reflects a dynamic and developmental view of psychology. A state of consciousness is not *what* a person thinks, but the underlying system of needs, desires, and the degree of psycho-spiritual development that determines *why* he thinks and acts as he does. This definition reflects an interest in the overall mode of human functioning, physically and psychologically.

The doctrines of transcendent humanism and emergent evolutionism combine to provide an image of man which is at once faithful to both the scientific view that humanity is the product of an evolutionary process and the religious or philosophical intuition that we possess an underlying spiritual nature. I will argue, in fact, that evolution is working towards a kind of spiritual perfection in man. Further, we can enhance this process, becoming an *agent,* rather than simply a *product* of evolution. The implications of this for society are clear. We must foster this developmental process by modifying social institutions and, indeed, the underlying purpose of social order itself. This will entail a paradigm shift from our current emphasis on the production and acquisition of material products to an increased focus on self-actualization. I will argue that, to a great extent, the social and psychological problems of our current era are symptoms of the frustration of this underlying need to progress, as individuals and as a society, to a higher level of existence.

In the end I may have to yield to the charge that this work is something of a tract. What I have projected for future man is as much prescriptive as it is descriptive. My belief that what *will be* and what *may be* are not coextensive underscores the following pages line by line. I write in the hope that we will exercise wisdom and tolerance in shaping the best of all possible future worlds out of today's actual world, and that I might offer some thoughts to help the seeker answer his most basic questions.

Finally, allow me to apologize for my exclusive use of the masculine pronoun and the generalization "mankind" or simply "man." In the trend to become gender neutral, our language can be awkward and unmanageable. I have deferred to the dictates of readability in this matter, but mean no disparagement of women.

I

Philosophy and Mind

1
The Philosophy of Enlightenment

The story comes down to us that the philosopher Bertrand Russell took an almost immediate interest in his later calling. Even at a very early age he was beset with the symptoms of the "why" syndrome, the single most characteristic sign of the would-be philosopher. This condition is marked by long periods of silent introspection followed by equally long chains of precocious questions, the answer to each eliciting from the child-interrogator the irreverent response, "But why?" In an effort to discourage his youthful proclivity to metaphysics in favor of a more respectable profession, Russell's Victorian grandmother would muse, "What is mind? No matter. What is matter? Never mind."

The problem of the relationship between mind (or spirit, soul, consciousness) and matter (including the material brain) has been perhaps the most fundamental problem facing thinkers down through history. This is so because the mind-body problem speaks to what we are most essentially as sentient beings. The solutions given to our deepest and most burning questions will depend largely upon the answer given to the more fundamental mind-body problem. Is there life after death? Are we free to choose as we wish, or are all decisions the product of neural (brain) processes? What does it mean to "be aware"?

These and other such issues cannot be answered without first answering the problem of the relationship between mind and body.

Though it is oversimplifying the picture somewhat, one can say that the mind-body problem has been answered in two fundamentally different ways through the history of philosophy. The first position, known as "dualism," holds that mind (or soul) and body are two distinct substances, that mind may exist independently of the body and, consequently, that life after death is possible. A majority of the great traditional religions posit a dualist conception of mind and body. The promise of an afterlife, as characteristic of Christianity, Islam, Hinduism, and various polytheistic forms of religion, is absolutely contingent on holding some sort of dualistic view. In contrast, original Buddhism did not posit a soul that survives death, as evidenced by the doctrine of *anatta* (no soul).

Most dualists believe that the mind or soul—the two are not always seen as identical—interacts with the brain and the material body, allowing the mind to influence bodily behavior. Thus, the mind has an influence in the material world. At the same time, however, the mind is not bound to the material world. For example, upon the death of the body, the mind would presumably carry on in one or another state. Each of the various religions, of course, has its own particular doctrines explaining what becomes of the soul at this time.

The second major position taken to solve the mind-body problem is known by a variety of different terms, each of which has slightly differing implications. Before I can develop the view put forth in this book, it is necessary to touch on two related concepts, naturalism and materialism. Broadly speaking, one can be a naturalist without being a materialist, but all materialists are naturalists: materialism is one form of naturalism. In the twentieth century the two concepts have been largely equated with one another. This is because materialism is the majority view among philosophers and scientists in this century. Nonetheless, one can be a naturalist without being a (reductionistic) materialist. In fact, naturalism (without reductionism) is the view that is the basis of this book. It is helpful to understand something of this position before going on to the discussions of enlightenment and its effect on society.

Naturalism, with respect to the mind-body problem, might be simplified to express one major hypothesis:

1) Thoughts, awareness, or mentality in animals and man have arisen as a result of a natural evolutionary process, are dependent on the physical brain for their continued existence, and consequently cannot survive the death of the body.

Reductionistic materialism, however, adds a second hypothesis:

2) Not only are thoughts, perceptions, and all forms of mentality dependent upon physical brain processes; in fact they are identical with these brain processes. Consequently, thoughts cannot have an effect on the physical world. Instead, they are merely byproducts of brain processes or, by some views, another way of *talking about* brain processes.

There is a wealth of literature on the subject of philosophy of mind, and the area has become so complicated that as short an explication as attempted here can serve only to simplify the issues for the interested layman, and to set the stage for the investigation of enlightenment as a factor in evolution, which follows in this book. (Those interested in further investigating the issues and various materialistic theories of mind should see the appendix.)

Dualism has traditionally entertained a more inspiring view of the nature of man than has naturalism. The belief that the soul of man is indestructible has the subtle effect of expanding the possibilities for the human condition, not only in the afterlife, but here on earth as well. Conversely, the view that human existence is of a limited, finite scope intimately touches the way we perceive our innermost nature, the meaning of our existence, and the scope of our potential. While this need not have been the case, the rise of naturalism has had a chilling effect on our view of ourselves as spiritual beings. Materialism, in particular, has been ubiquitously associated with the alleged decline of modern morals, the decay of filial order, and the current existential malaise which now confronts mankind in all post-modern industrial societies.

Perhaps man's greatest shortcoming is his inability to confront his own mortality. Insofar as the naturalistic world view underscores the fact that we are finite beings, that we will not live forever, it is associated with, and perhaps responsible for, our modern lack of spiritual fulfillment. Presumably, the argument goes something like this: "If I can't live forever, nothing I do now can matter in any ultimate sense. Without a sense of ultimacy, the mundane, day to day, is completely without meaning. Therefore, life itself is devoid of significance." Indeed, this appears to be the argument of a wide spectrum of pessimistic existential thinkers who have gained ascendency in the present century.

However, naturalism need not have such pernicious effects. Modern man is a seed of what he might become. Acknowledging our mortality, our dependence, and the importance of our sheer contingency is the first step in realizing our ultimate potential as spiritual beings. What is needed is a new view of the human condition, complete with a basic metaphysical and psychological outlook. The concept of what I will call "psycho-spiritual development" is not inconsistent with a broadly naturalistic world view, as will be shown.

Emergent Evolutionism: Naturalism without Reductionism

The true reductionist holds that all sciences ultimately can be reduced to physics. For example, psychology can be reduced to biology, by this view. Biology itself can be reduced to the laws of chemistry, which in turn are completely reducible to fundamental physical laws. Thus, everything in the universe, from the most complex human interaction to the reactions of subatomic particles, are all explainable by the same laws of physics.

There is a naturalistic alternative to reductionism called "emergent evolutionism." This view allows for the appearance of surprises and novel developments in evolution. The great gestalt psychologist Wolfgang Kohler commented:

> Emergent evolution . . . cannot be defended without attacking physics at the same time. On the other hand, if the physicist is right, no place is left for new principles which suddenly take over—when systems become particularly complicated. The concept of emergent evolution does not appeal to the scientific mind. We will see later, however, that most attempts to deal with the mind-body problem tacitly accept other forms of emergence (Kohler 1939, 23).

The alternative to reductionistic naturalism, then, appears to be predicated on this notion of emergence. This position can lead to a more inspiring and hopeful view of human nature than reductionism has. Let me exemplify what this means. Suppose that science knew all there is to know about hydrogen atoms in isolation. Further, suppose we gained all knowledge of oxygen atoms. Thus we would know what each atom is composed of and what all of its characteristic properties are in isolation. Emergent evolutionary theory holds that even so, science would never be able to predict that combining hydrogen and oxygen in a certain way would result in a substance with the properties of water. Liquid properties are qualitatively different from gaseous properties; when they arose they introduced an altogether new state of matter in the universe.

Take another example. Modern astrophysics tells us that for the first one hundred thousand years of its existence, the universe contained no matter, only energy. If scientists could have been present at that time, even if they were privy to all pertinent information, they could not have predicted that properties such as solidity, extension, and color would come on the scene. Matter is an *emergent* property, proceeding from the unstable fields of energy which completely constituted the young universe.

Similarly, mind is not strictly identical with matter in the sense that a thought *is* the concomitant brain process. Rather, mind or mental properties emerged from matter. The eminent English philosopher C.D. Broad held this view, which he termed "emergent materialism." This view, he writes, asserts: "a) materiality is a differentiating structure, and b) that mentality is an emergent characteristic" (Broad 1925, 646). By "differentiating structure" Broad simply means that "matter" may be manifested in a wide spectrum of properties, some not being "material" in the usual sense. This opens the way for the emergence of ever-developing human qualities.

The view of emergent evolution is unpopular in much of the scientific world because it suggests that we know much less about the world than we supposed. It is soothing for the scientist to admit that, though it is now unforseeable, higher-level sciences such as psychology will one day be theoretically reducible to physics. It is less comfortable to acknowledge that the science of physics covers only a small portion of the spectrum of reality. To this point, the inability of scientists successfully to reduce psychological laws to physical ones has been met by an attitude of "wait and see." This reduction may be practically impossible at this point in time, but it remains theoretically possible. This attitude has often characterized the view of the scientific hegemony just before some cherished paradigm crumbled.

C.D. Broad writes:

> On the emergent theory we have to reconcile ourselves to much less unity in the external world and a much less intimate connection between the various sciences. At best, the external world and the various sciences that deal with it will form a kind of hierarchy. We might, if we like, keep the view that there is only one fundamental kind of stuff (Broad 1925, 77).

This is exactly the view that I am proposing. In my view, what are commonly called "energy," "matter," and "mind" are simply different states, manifested by different sets of properties, of one fundamental substance. This view is "physicalistic" only in the sense that it holds that there are naturally occurring and ultimately knowable law-like relationships among these different states, and that, in the case of the living world, what is considered "mental" is existentially dependent on the lower physical level for its continued existence.

In his book *Science and Moral Priority,* one of this century's greatest brain scientists, Roger Sperry, outlines a similar view. He writes rejecting dualism:

> Advances of the mind-brain sciences of the past few decades have very substantially narrowed the latitude for speculation. In particular, the accumulating evidence in neuroscience leads overwhelmingly today to the conviction that conscious mental awareness is a property of, and inseparably tied to, the living brain. This is something that modern science points to as a salient reality of our world that we must now face. . . . A concept of mind and matter emerges that supports a unifying this-world view of man in nature (Sperry 1983, 21).

Sperry also rejects reductionism, a move which he says places him in a minority of .1% of all neurophysiologists. In the reductionistic view:

> Consciousness, in the objective approach, is clearly made a second-rate citizen in the causal picture. It is relegated to the inferior status of an inconsequential byproduct, an epiphenomenon, or most commonly, just an inner aspect of the one material brain process (Sperry 1983, 29).

In full accord with the view propounded in this book, Sperry writes: "By our current mind-brain theory, monism has to include subjective mental properties as causal realities" (Sperry 1983, 79). By making this move, Sperry rejects the idea that it is the physical correlates of thought that are causally efficacious in behavior. Instead, consciousness itself enters into the causal chain of sensation to decision to the resultant behavior. This leaves room for free will and man's intervention in his own evolution, as will be discussed.

If we view the process of evolution as a series of hierarchically structured levels, each level with its separate system of properties, processes, and laws, along with a group of transordinal laws which connect the various levels (mind and matter, for example), we glimpse a picture of reality that transcends the extremes of dualism and reductionism. Further, it appears that each higher level of evolution may have a dominant downward control over the more subordinate levels. For example, if mental properties have emerged from matter, then it seems plausible that, in the evolutionary scheme, mind is greatly dependent on matter at the lower levels of evolution. For example the behavior of one-celled organisms in which mental processes are confined to very rudimentary stimulus-response relationships may be largely explainable in physical terms. At these lower levels causality works mostly from physical to mental. But as mind develops in higher animals and in man, it begins to have a dominant effect on the physical processes in the body. Thus the flow of causality "switches" from physical-to-mental to mental-to-physical. The mental moves from the position of dependent to independent variability. Sperry likens this ever-increasing supervenience of higher properties on lower ones to the way the individual atoms and molecules in a wheel are carried along, irrespective of their individual movements, by the greater movement of the rolling wheel. Further, he writes:

> When it comes to brains, remember that the simpler electric, atomic, molecular, and cellular forces and laws, though still present and operating, have been superseded by the configurational forces of higher level mechanisms. At the powers of perception, cognition, reason, judgement, and the like, the operational, causal effects and forces are equally or more potent in

brain dynamics than are the outclassed inner chemical forces (Sperry 1983, 88).

Emergent evolutionism, then, is a naturalistic theory insofar as it holds that mentality originally arose from physical states in the history of evolution. Further, these mental states are contingent on brain processes for their continued existence. At the same time, however, mental states can exert a "downward" causal influence on the material processes of the brain, thus vindicating the commonsense judgment that thoughts have a causal influence on real-world action. The theory is even more interesting, however, in its psycho-spiritual implications. If it is true that evolution manifests itself on many levels and is not limited to the Darwinian sense of the term, and if it is operating in the human species at the level of mentality, perhaps evolution can be enhanced, augmented, or guided by our own actions. The theme that humankind may take part in advancing and directing the course of its own subsequent evolution will run through this book.

In what direction might this process take us? One powerful suggestion, made by R.M. Bucke, the author of *Cosmic Consciousness,* among others, is that evolution in man is now working on a higher level towards psycho-spiritual development. Qualities such as altruism, compassion, heightened intellectual ability, increased emotional sensitivity, and unshakable equanimity of mind all have survival value in a world such as ours, threatened by nuclear war, international strife, political and economic inequality, as well as a host of various social and psychological maladies. These are also the qualities reported to be enhanced by meditation and other forms of psycho-spiritual self-discipline.

Philosophy and the Western Search for the Self

Eastern philosophy is usually credited with advancing explanations for transcendent states and higher realms of human potential. However, there are compelling parallels between Eastern and Western philosophy that are often overlooked. Some of the West's most profound systems of ideas suggest a deep understanding of human potential. Further, some of the greatest Western philosophers not only had insights into these higher realms but may have used meditation, contemplation, or other systems of psycho-spiritual development to experience subjectively these more profound states of consciousness. Before examining these philosophers and their concepts, it is necessary to take a brief look at two trends in Western philosophy.

From its inception, Western philosophy has been the arena for a curious battle between two fundamentally opposed ways of thinking about reality. These are known as "rationalism" and "empiricism." Basically, the distinction between the two can be seen in the differing conception each school has for man's relationship with the external world. Rationalism, at least in its extreme form, holds that certitude, truth and knowledge all are in some sense to be found in man himself. The world of the intellect is primary while the sensory world is not to be trusted, an unreliable appearance which does not convey truth or reality. The spirit of rationalism holds that at some level man, by thinking, contemplating, or intuiting, may come to realize external truths. A weaker version of this doctrine is that external reality is completely understandable, though the answers themselves are not innate. The empiricist, on the other hand, holds that knowledge can be gained only from the external, sensuous world. Further, all appearances of necessity in the world, either in the form of causal laws or a priori truths, are trivial or contentious.

It is plain, even from this brief description of each, that rationalism lends itself more easily to mystical interpretation. Conversely, it has been the province of twentieth-century analytic philosophy largely to reject rationalism as a romanticization. Though the doctrines of rationalism and idealism should not be confused, there is usually a similarity of approach between the two. Finally, it should be noted that these doctrines far transcend traditional philosophy and can be seen even in various psychological, sociological, and historical schools of thought. Thus Jung falls easily into the realm of the rationalist with his concept of the archetype, while the behaviorist Skinner upholds a radical form of empiricism with his "black box" concept of the mind.

A look at the august lineage of Western philosophers reveals time and again the search for or actual insights into a psychological state that far transcends everyday consciousness. There were both metaphysical and epistemological reasons for this quest. The road of empiricism ultimately leads to solipsism, the view that nothing in the world has an existence independent of oneself. Rationalism, on the other hand, could not defend its notions of logical and causal necessity against the attack of skepticism. A number of important philosophers, generally rationalists, began to erect a bridge from the realm of the intellect to a different realm altogether—an intuitive, even mystical, approach to reality. Consequently, the concept of enlightenment is not limited to the esoteric thinkers of various Oriental cultures. Though current scholars have either failed to recognize or have outright denied it, the greatest thinkers of the West have entertained similar notions.

Nowhere is this more obvious than in the works of Plato. It is common knowledge that Plato was heavily influenced by Pythagorean mysticism and may have practiced a form of contemplative meditation. Plato not only makes a metaphysical statement about true reality, but is also concerned with the psychological question: By what means may man become acquainted with the Real? His allegory of the cave is a demonstration of this. Plato envisions a cave wherein a number of prisoners are chained facing a wall. They are able to look only forward. On the wall in front of them shadows are projected by puppeteers from a gallery behind the inmates. Having spent their lives in this manner, the prisoners take the shadows to be the real things of the world. Plato remarks that the scientists among them would construct theories about the movements of the shadows, and all would speculate as to their nature. Were a prisoner to be freed and dragged out of the cave into the world of real objects, he would be forever changed. After becoming accustomed to bright sunlight, the once-prisoner would see trees, birds, and all those things of which the real world is made. Further, if the freed man were to return to the cave in an attempt to enlighten the other inmates, they would take him for insane and violently resist any effort to be freed. Plato's allegory is no mere fable of the process of conventional education. His language suggests that this is a tale of enlightenment in the most significant sense of the word. The venturer is permanently changed by his "rising of the soul into the world of mind" (Plato 1956, 312-16). He is no longer attracted to the realm of shadows—fame, money, and sensuous pleasures are poor substitutes for one who has seen the sun.

Later philosophers allude to lesser states of mind wherein one attains a contemplative peace or evenness through all of his activities. Aristotle's *eudaimonia* and the Stoics *euthymia* are examples of this. Achievement of these states of mind brings an autonomy to one's life, a centeredness which is unshakable.

It is in the writings of Plotinus, however, that a form of mysticism and philosophy strikingly similar to that of the Vedas of India can be found. Plotinus' conception of the One of reality, along with his contention that true self-knowledge arises only when the subject, the act of thinking, and the object of thought become unified, could have been the pronouncement of a Shankara. Unlike the lives of other Western philosophers, there is little question among scholars that Plotinus was not simply speaking abstractly, but in fact experienced states of unity consciousness. He considered these, the result of the practice of "unthinking thinking," as the goal of all life. Plotinus' blend of Neoplatonism with mystic theosophy stands as one of the most unique syntheses of abstract philosophy and experiential practice known to the West.

A great many other philosophers and sages of the Middle Ages have been documented as having similar types of transitions from the abstract to the experiential. Not only are there the ecstasies of Meister Eckhart, St. Teresa of Avila, St. John of the Cross, but no less a philosopher and scholar than Thomas Aquinas confessed that the insights he had gained as a result of such experiences were worth more than all his voluminous writings combined.

In modern times it was the philosopher Spinoza who seems to have rekindled the light of a different state of consciousness. Though Spinoza's philosophy is fundamentally rationalistic and deterministic, it moves beyond this in a number of profound ways. Spinoza, who has been called everything from the "atheist Jew" to "that God-intoxicated man," posits a monism of substance which includes all of nature. His God, which is equated with nature, is an immanent, nontranscendent, nonpersonal God. Everything in nature is a part or "mode" of the one substance that is God. But God has many "attributes," the two known to men being mind and matter. (Spinoza holds there are an infinite number of other such attributes.) Accordingly, there is a strict parallelism between occurrences under the different attributes of matter and mind. For example, we can look at any human action in two different ways. When a man is observed to get up from his desk for a glass of water, we can explain his action in strictly physico-chemical terms, as a scientist would, as independent of thought. Or we can view his action in terms of the desire for water, the need to quench the thirst, and the thought as to how this can be done, all of which are mental acts. Thus essentially one event has two different levels of explanation respective to the attributes of mind and matter, or what Spinoza calls "thought" and "extension."

Though he countenanced no personal God, Spinoza was a deeply spiritual man. He sought, within the framework of naturalistic philosophy, to give humankind a sense of the sacred, of what has in certain theistic orientations been called "blessedness." Spinoza's "intellectual love of God" is a state wherein the individual becomes resigned to the deterministic necessity of all the world, but rejoices in the possibility of understanding nature (God). At this stage one becomes free of the human bondage which is endemic of the ignorant. There is a marked similarity between this, Spinoza's view of virtue, and Plato's *arete*. In both views true knowledge is an absolute prerequisite to moral goodness and psychological contentment. There is also an interesting parallel between both of these views and the Hindu concept of gaining freedom from karma, the result of the pursuit of a detached though all-understanding approach to all of one's activities. By this view, the subject acts in accord with the laws of nature (or the three Gunas of Hindu philosophy) and has become master over oneself by being detached from the consequences of all action. One acts understandingly, selflessly, and contentedly in all life's pursuits. The parallel here breaks down, however, in that in Eastern accounts of liberation self-realization is accompanied by genuine freedom; "the bonds of karma" fall forever from the enlightened soul. For Spinoza, one never steps outside the strictly deterministic network of causes and effects, but instead learns to act in accordance with these laws. Thus, one is free in the sense that one acts in harmony with what must necessarily be.

Though Spinoza's quest for peace of soul was cast largely in rationalistic terms, some have interpreted him as a man with a deeper insight who was constrained by the language of the scientist and philosopher to speak of basically intuitive or transcendental insights in a rationalistic way. Thus, some have pointed to what he has deemed the highest goal of human life as a transrational pursuit, the exercise of reason being a means to an extrarational end. Whether Spinoza ever experienced so-called mystical or transcendental interludes is a matter of some controversy, though his life singularly stands as an example of one of the few Western thinkers who practiced what he preached. He was, as Bertrand Russell said, "the noblest of the philosophers."

Other Western systems of philosophy have interesting parallels to a number of themes central to various Eastern systems. The two most worthy of note here are those of Descartes and Kant.

In his famous pronouncement "I think, therefore I am," Descartes reaffirms a basic contention of the *Upanishads* that epistemological certainty rests solely with the subjective, or the "Atman." Descartes' dictum should be understood in a wider sense than is often described by Western philosophers. The "I think" is not the speculative, intellectualized, limited notion of reason associated with problem-solving and creative thinking. Rather, Descartes should be understood to have meant, "I am introspectively aware, therefore I am." In other words, while the external world is known with less than epistemological certainty, there is no way I can be deluded in that I am aware, I feel, and I think. Everything external is filtered through the subjective principle; thus, subjective awareness is epistemologically prior to the world.

Kant is also concerned with the relation between subject and object, noumenon and phenomenon. A fundamental problem to Kantian philosophy may be paraphrased as the Upanishadic "How may the knower be known?" We have never seen the subject. Rather, the subject stands behind all objective reality: we could not know the object without the subject. However, as Hume pointed out, "I can never catch my *self.* Whenever I try, I always stumble on some sense impression or idea." Kant's work is an attempt to reconcile Humean skepticism with the existence of a transcendent self. Kovoor Behanan, an Indian historian of philosophy, evaluates the relationship between Kantian and yogic thought:

> The "I think" is the necessary condition of the higher "Unity of Apperception." The consciousness of self, although implied in all experience, need not always be actually realized; it may remain hovering in the dim background as a potentiality capable of realization.

> This is the Pure Ego to which he [Kant] gave the name "original transcendental synthetic Unity of Apperception." Kant, like the yogic philosophers, knew perfectly well the utter futility of any attempt to explore the nature of such a quality-less soul. We could not even know whether it is material or immaterial, simple or substantial. Since it is beyond our introspection, Kant admitted that psychology could gain nothing by this metaphysical entity; instead, the empirical "Me" should constitute its proper subject matter. In the language of yoga, Kant's empirical "Me" would correspond to the individual buddhi and its manifestations. But the Pure Ego of Kant and the transcendental purusha [of yoga], both dim barren abstractions, look very much like two peas from the same pod (Behanan 1937, 59).

The work of a number of the nineteenth-century idealists, from Hegel to Bradley, also portrays the overt influence of the Orient on Western philosophy. While twentieth-century positivism has been the result of a deliberate reaction against the idealism of the previous century, and though contemporary academic philosophy has put as much ground as possible between itself and what it considers to be the romantic obscurantism of this earlier time, the influences of rationalism and idealism can be found in many twentieth-century psychological theories just the same. Particularly in psychoanalysis and most notably in the work of Freud and Jung, idealistic metaphysics is alive and well (see Chapter Two).

Three Views of the Self: Ego, Soul and Atman

If it is true, as Maslow has said, that "We are neurotic to the extent that we are self-less," then our basic priority must surely be to search for, find, or develop this thing called "self." It should come as no surprise, then, that an exploration of the topic of enlightenment is intimately intertwined with a discussion of selfhood. Indeed, these may be two paths to the same goal. To be enlightened, whatever else this term designates, surely entails the knowledge of what one most fundamentally *is*. And this is exactly the problem of the self.

In the history of philosophy East and West, there are three broad notions of what man basically is, what constitutes the self: soul, atman, and ego. These correspond roughly with the concepts of man held by the religions of the West, the religions of the East, and the modern scientific outlook, respectively. It is interesting to examine these in relation to what they contribute to our understanding of enlightenment.

The most familiar of these views to the Western reader is the concept of the individual everlasting soul central to the Judeo-Christian and Islamic traditions. By this view, the true self is separate from the material body and is thus immaterial and permanent. In attempting to discern exactly what this soul is or what its properties are, we are given two broad types of answers: it is that which is responsible for animating the body, for producing life in the otherwise inanimate material husk; and/or it is identical with the mind, or with those activities we commonly designate as mental.

The first and more primitive of these concepts is the soul-as-animator theory. By this view, the soul animates the otherwise inanimate body. What distinguishes the animate from the inanimate, the living from the nonliving or dead, is the presence of the soul, so that it is at least a necessary condition for life. Plato seems to have held a view similar to this.

The first problem with this view becomes apparent as a result of the modern medical understanding of the human body. Put simply, science can explain the workings of the various bodily functions as interactions of physical and chemical processes. An extra "soul component" is not needed to understand the operations of the heart, lungs, brain, and the overall physiological system. This, of course, does not prove that there is no soul. It simply suggests that whatever else the soul does, it is not necessary to the continued operation of the physical body.

A second problem results when the soul-as-animator view is combined with the Christian contention that only human beings have souls. Logically, if existence of a soul is necessary for life, and if man is the only creature with a soul, then man is the only living creature. But this is not true, of course. Plants and animals are also living beings, as distinct from the inanimate world of rocks and minerals. To hold the soul-as-animator theory consistently, one must allow that all other living creatures—including one-celled organisms, plants, and animals—also have souls. Or, consistently to hold that only man has a soul logically entails that the soul has some other function than that of an animating force.

The soul-as-animator theory has largely been abandoned by modern philosophers and theologians in favor of a more sophisticated view. This second alternative views the soul as equivalent to mind or consciousness. The holder of this theory might maintain that the physical body can live on in a vegetative state without the soul, as in cases of irreversible coma, but that conscious awareness, or at least some form of mental activity, is dependent upon the presence of the soul.

The first problem with this theory is similar to the major difficulty with the soul-as-animator view. Briefly, modern science and medicine have demonstrated the dependence of mind on the physical body. Memory, perception, cognition, and all other mental activities are brain-dependent. For example, experiments have been conducted wherein one laboratory rat is trained to perform a particular task. Then part of this animal's brain is surgically removed and implanted into the brain of a second rat. This second untrained animal then performs the task which the first had learned. This reveals that memory patterns of the former have been transferred to the latter, implying that memory resides in the physical brain, not in an immaterial soul. Like other mental functions, memory is limited. It fades with time and deteriorates with the coming of old age. Perception and sensation are likewise contingent on the proper functioning of bodily components. Even the greatest of human functions by which man separates himself from the remainder of the animal kingdom—intellect—is answerable to physical cause and effect. For these reasons, it becomes increasingly difficult to credit an immaterial soul, equivalent to mind or consciousness, with such prodigious shortcomings. What soul-ful memory is this that a bump on the skull can remove? What immaterial rationality, shared by God and man alone, can be the victim of a degenerative cancer? In short, no immortal soul can be imperiled by physical injury.

Descartes attempted to avoid this problem and reconcile soul with science by holding that the soul interacts with the physical body through the pineal gland. Thus physical damage could bring about mental loss without disturbing the soul. But on this view, what is left of the soul? If all mental functioning is brain-based rather than soul-based, as suggested, then we are left with a soul with unknown properties, which cannot remember, think, sense, or carry out any other mental function. No disembodied soul could remember its past life, its past loves, or, for that matter, anything about itself. Such an existence surely would not pose a satisfactory alternative to death's complete annihilation of the individual.

Long before these metaphysical difficulties were stumbled across in the West, the East had accepted these and other similar problems connected with the soul-as-mind theory. It is to the overall credit of the Oriental philosopher that he long ago accepted the discontinuity of *buddhi* (mind) and *purusha* (soul).

The Eastern concept of soul is that which is pure subjectivity or pure consciousness. It is no object, but rather illuminates all objects through the empirical mind. Mind, as such, contains all of the sense impressions Hume discussed, the ideas of "myself." But these are not what is most basic to *me*, the Easterner explains. If I am simply the momentary feelings, thoughts, and impressions that I loosely entertain, then what I am dies with the passing of each thought. If I am identical with my present mood, then as the mood dies, so do I. "But there is something behind the mood, the idea, or the impression," the Westerner will argue. "Precisely, the point!" says the Easterner, and commences to explain what this something is. Basically, it is that passive substance that observes all of the objects of the world. In some cases it identifies with these objects and they are mistaken for the self. At other times these objects are seen as something wholly other.

Behanan writes:

> [The self] is the eternal seer behind the phenomena of prakrita (matter) and its changes. It is without parts and attributes, all pervasive and subtle. Whatever it may be that characterizes individuality, the empirical "me" is of the essence of prakriti, and purusha contributes nothing to the sum total of personality. This inactive, characterless purusha may be put down on the positive side as pure consciousness. . . . This is the transcendent principle of consciousness, purusha, the never-changing soul that makes the content of the mind meaningful. Samkhya Yoga admits that this factor cannot clearly be observed in introspection which reveals only the mental film-roll, but not the light (consciousness) that enables the picture to be registered. The presence of this purusha as a theoretically necessary principle may be safely inferred from the data of knowledge. One can only wonder at this point if it is Kant or the Samkha yoga who is speaking (Behanan 1937, 43-44).

This concept of *purusha* or *atman* provides little solace to those awaiting an afterlife on that eternal spring afternoon, to the laughter of loved ones and the sound of harps. No such reality can be countenanced by these tough-minded mystics. Rather, the afterlife is an empty interlude devoid of personality between lives, a time in the void of an unconscious purgatory. But if there is no personality, quality, or aspect of the individual soul or atman, it will be asked, what exactly distinguishes *me* from *you*? If both you and I are, at bottom, a personality-less, quality-less state of pure consciousness, what distinguishes my pure subjectivity from yours? This is a point of great controversy in the East.

In the *Upanishads,* atman, the subjective element, and Brahman, the objective side of reality, are identical. Thus all souls are part of one great soul:

> I am Brahman. Atman is Brahman. . . . The self and the not-self are equally manifestations of the Absolute and are at bottom one. The individual self is, in fact, no longer individual, but universal (Sharma 1960, 26).

The Samkhya-yogic philosopher, however, does not agree. Though the highest goal of life is union with God, union implies distinctness. Thus, for the latter group, individual souls are separate both from one another and from God.

The concept of self as atman or pure consciousness can be looked at in another way. In Western philosophy metaphysicians are commonly confronted with the problem of substance versus property. The problem can be roughly formulated as follows: In talking about any object, we describe it by listing its various properties or attributes. We say "The pin cushion is soft, large, blue," and list the numerous properties of a thing. But this manner of speech suggests that there is something about the pin cushion *beyond* its properties like softness, largeness, blueness. When we say "The pin cushion is blue," we seem to suggest that there is something more to the pin cushion than its properties. We talk about the pin cushion as if it were something substantial in which the various properties inhere. This is the Western notion of substance, an important part of the metaphysics of Aristotle, Descartes, and virtually all other rationalists.

This way of talking is also used in describing ourselves. We say, "I am angry," or "I am five feet, ten." We speak as if there is some "I" more fundamental than the properties "angry," or "five feet, ten." It is precisely this intuition that has led the mystic to posit a spiritual substance more fundamental than the various accidental physical and mental properties we use to describe ourselves. And it is this fundamental spiritual essence, analogous to the rationalist's substance, that is the atman or pure consciousness for the mystic. It is that which is beyond attribution, Kant's noumenon, and the very core of human identity for the Oriental philosopher. Since this spiritual core is beyond all attributes, we cannot say anything meaningful about it. Yet, the mystic maintains, it is what gives us our sense of identity through all of the diverse experiences we encounter.

All empiricists, including most modern psychologists, reject the concept of substance. For this group, the pin cushion simply is the conpresence of all those properties —blue, soft, large, etc.—by which we describe it. There is nothing more. Substance is, as Hume said, an "unintelligible chimera." Similarly, most modern psychologists reject the notion of the indescribable atman. For them the self is simply a combination of those properties, processes, and experiences we subjectively experience through introspection. This is the modern concept of ego.

It is a common quip in philosophical circles that modern psychology first lost its soul, then lost its mind, and finally became completely unconscious. This saying reflects the disdain that many from diverse orientations—humanists, theists, and others—have had for the self-annihilating influence of much of modern psychology. This is an apt portrayal when it is realized that no mainstream modern theory of personality countenances an immortal soul. In this view all psychological attributes—intelligence, honesty, forgiveness, etc.—are explained in terms of diverse and separate psychological functions or dispositions. This program is then often mapped onto a materialism that understands different intellectual and emotional capacities and dispositions as being products of various parts of the brain. There was no function left for the soul except to calm the minds of the existentially distressed with the belief that an afterlife does indeed lie ahead, despite all evidence to the contrary. In this manner, the soul was ousted as an ontological constituent unnecessary to psychology.

However, if there is no soul, to what do we attribute the feeling of "self-ness"? What is responsible for self-awareness, or for a belief in subject-as-opposed-to-object, as well as for the feeling of identity through time? Modern psychology answers in a rational manner. The presence of self-awareness is a self-construction or interpretation of the mind *by* the mind. At one moment Smith behaves in a way which, when he looks back at it a moment later, elicits pride, embarrassment, disgust, or some other reaction in accordance with certain socially internalized standards and patterns of behavior. There is no one subjective self, but rather a continuous river of seeing-oneself-in-such-and-such a situation, acting in such-and-such a manner, and assessing that behavior in accordance with various internalized standards. As such, every conceivable mental reification such as conscience intelligence or will can be explained by various psychophysiological functions and interactions between these functions. Different theories have different models as to what these structures of personality are and how they interact, but for all such theories, without exception, there is no central core of the personality that is ontologically or temporally prior to the rest of the personality. D.M. Armstrong has suggested, for example, that self-consciousness is a construct that is intimately tied to memory, and that the loss of the latter will entail the demise of the former (Armstrong 1980, 59-67).

If, by the Western conception, there is no central subject, what is the function of the ego or the self in so many modern theories of personality? It is basically the illusory psychological place-holder for all subjective experience, or for one's capacities and dispositions, or for all that takes place in consciousness. To be sure, no two theorists seem to share exactly the same view of the self or ego. Further, some posit both a self *and* an ego, contrasting the two psychic elements. Others use the term "ego" to denote what still others have called "self," and vice versa. In any event, theories of selfhood are a dime-a-dozen in the wholesale conceptual bakery that is modern psychology. Despite these differences, however, all of these views are similar in that: 1) The self or ego is not innate or present at birth at least as it is experienced in normal adulthood, but rather develops as a result of one or another set of processes. 2) It is not permanent, but rather changes with time and circumstance. A direct consequence of this view is that 3) The self does not survive death. It is a psycho-physiological construction which fades to black with the demise of the organism.

It is obvious even after this cursory sketch of the three different views of human identity that the contrast among them is absolutely insurmountable. By one notion, the mark of human selfhood is, fundamentally, immortality. For another, it is immortality, pure subjectivity, and universalizability. All souls are intertwined in what amounts to an Oversoul, a cosmic unity of souls. For the first view, realization of selfhood occurs basically at the time of death. For the second view, a long series of lives and deaths may be necessary before the true self is realized. For the last view, the development and realization of the self is the inevitable result of intersocial and/or intrapersonal interaction. It is no stable entity, but rather a reification, a psychological construction, a hypostatization that comprises a labile river whose continued course is contingent upon the health of the physical body.

In the chapters that follow, a naturalistic and humanistic conception of the self will be elaborated, but one distinct from the various ego theories just discussed. The solution will accord the experience of pure consciousness an important place in our notion of self-development, but at the same time will place this experience in a scientific "this worldly" context.

The Future of Philosophy

What must modern philosophy do to regain its rightful place as the systematizer of knowledge and the liberator of mankind? It must begin by wilfully addressing the questions of most importance to human beings. It must recognize that such questions as How can life be lived most meaningfully? are not mere "empirical" questions, condescendingly relegated to psychologists, sociologists, and political scientists. These are questions that must be addressed unflinchingly, in the light of past confusions, failings, and prejudices. These are the enduring questions; they transcend everything else. All the world changes, but these fundamental issues remain. The ancient Greek and the modern cosmopolitan face the selfsame problems: In what way is this finite existence most meaningfully spent? What values are most worthy of being embraced to secure this prescribed good life? It is these questions to which we owe our attention—indeed our allegiance—and in failing to answer them, philosophy fails its purpose, its tradition, and fails humanity itself. In short, step one in the rejuvenation of philosophy must be to accord these questions the primacy they demand, regardless of the answers we may have given in the past.

The second action philosophy must take is to eschew its disdain for consideration of all things empirical. A word of explanation might be necessary here. Though contemporary philosophy is influenced by the scientific method, which explains its empirical orientation, philosophy largely avoids dealing with the *content* or results of modern science. Insofar as empirical phenomena are contingent, talking about the results of particular experiments is not essential to what the modern analytic philosopher perceives his task to be. This affliction is a prejudice equally affecting positivist and rationalist alike. Philosophy must reacquaint itself with the mortal plane, immersing itself in the study of relevant scientific, social, political, and economic developments. Perhaps the most salient example of what might be done for our purposes here is for the philosopher to take the lead in what other disciplines have called "consciousness exploration." That great rewards await as a result of such pursuits as meditation, biofeedback, and other systems of self-development is well documented and beyond empirical doubt. But the philosophical ramifications of consciousness research have not even begun to be examined. Modern philosophy already has the tools for such investigation. Phenomenological introspection provides the perfect—indeed the only—method for this undertaking. I am literally amazed that so little work has been done in this area by phenomenologists, both in elaborating the content of transcendent states of consciousness and in formulating general philosophical guidelines for investigation, in the spirit of Husserl.

As for philosophy generally, the various technologies for self-development and self-knowledge provide valuable insight into almost every area of philosophical inquiry. From ethics to the philosophy of mind, the fruits of such investigation would undoubtedly obliterate many conflicts and presuppositions characteristic of the modern Western world view. The modern philosopher must become the scientist in the laboratory of self-discovery; he must forge new modes of meaning and experience firsthand the phenomenon of self-integration. The philosopher, in short, must relinquish the arm chair for the world. He must never abandon his dedication to ideas, but must bring his ideas to the world, marshaling them for practical application in the quest for human fulfillment.

For philosophy to attain to the exalted position elaborated here, the modern philosopher must be an example of the very best that man can be. Life must become an aesthetic endeavor, and the life of the philosopher must become a picture at an exhibition. He must embody the virtues of freedom, wisdom, independence, and compassion, and must plainly exhibit these as inspiration for all. Incorporation of one or another mode of psycho-spiritual discipline in his life will be important in achieving the level of perfection required. But the need for discipline and development does not mean that life must be dull and ascetic, the product of a universal sublimation of worldly things to some otherworldly nirvana. Quite to the contrary, such a life can be filled with love and enjoyment, mischief and fun. In short, his life must become a celebration of his potential, and his potential is unlimited.

2
The Psychology of Enlightenment

In the captivating book *Living with the Himalayan Masters,* the Indian spiritual adept Swami Rama relates a conversation between himself and his venerated master. Swami Rama, still young and capricious, is about to leave for the West, and he asks his master if he should convert the Occident to the religion of the East. His master admonishes him, "Though these cultures [East and West] live in the same world with the same purpose of life, they are each extreme. Both East and West are still doing experiments on the right ways of living. The message of the Himalayan masters is timeless and has nothing to do with the primitive concepts of East and West. Extremes will not help humanity to attain the higher step of civilization for which we are all striving" (Rama 1978, 476-77).

Extreme though they may be, the past century has witnessed, at least at some levels, a reciprocal process where cultural divergencies merge and produce a moderating effect in respective societies. In the East the benefits of industrialization have found a waiting home. In the West, largely as a result of changes originating internally, a new world perspective has been slowly emerging.

It is as strange as it is true that in this century the scientist has largely become the mystic, while the philosopher has become the positivist, the materialist, and the logician. As physicist Irwin Schroedinger argued for the inseparability of subject and object, and no less formidable a biologist than C.H. Waddington was heard to echo assent to the *élan vital* of Bergson, leading men in the area of philosophy of mind have taken an opposite tack. On the more liberal side, it is routinely argued that the mental is ultimately and completely reducible to the physical, and on the more tough-minded side, that mental events do not exist at all! The work of Ryle, Smart, Skinner, and others attests to this fact.

There are, however, theories and claims, both Oriental and Occidental, that a greater level of psychological functioning is possible for humankind, and that this possibility, far from being potentially realized by only a chosen few, may be infused into society as a whole. There are trends in modern psychology that point to a transcendent, though still distinctly Western, view of humankind. A discussion of these more inspiring views of man's nature and potential follows.

Psychology and the Western Search for the Self

While twentieth-century Western philosophy has given up the ghost, so to speak, turning its back on the more fundamental spiritual and existential problems for a plethora of linguistic and logical considerations, modern psychoanalysis and humanistic psychology have taken up the search for the self, in what Ken Wilber has called "the atman project." Thus, the gap between philosophy and psychology in the West is, in certain respects, greater than ever. Modern analytic philosophy is not only physicalistic, but completely reductionistic as well. The traditional school of modern psychology which is most in sympathy with this view is behaviorism. Further, recent theories in modern cognitive science are also attempting to erect a bridge from the "mental language" of thoughts and feelings to the physical language of the natural scientist. But from a different corner of the world of psychology, a new movement is gaining impetus. Born of an interest in man's search for meaning and the post-positivistic conviction that psychology cannot be done in the manner of the natural sciences, another approach has become important. This is the third wave of psychology, or the humanistic approach.

While psychoanalysis has traditionally concerned itself with the psychologically troubled—the neurotic, psychotic, and a wide spectrum of psychopathology, and while behaviorism has set about determining the environmental contingencies in the study of the neurotic and the normal personality, humanistic psychology focuses on the highest potential for humankind. The study of the truly healthy personality, or what Maslow has called the "farther reaches of human nature," is its domain. Originally concerned with the psychological impact of various existential questions, including a profound interest in the process of finding meaning in life, these theorists have pointed to possibilities beyond the scope of "marginal man."

Before proceeding with these more contemporary of views, however, there is an older tradition that has in part contributed to the wealth of ideas fundamental to those operative in the third wave. Psychoanalysis, psychology's first wave, which first propounded the doctrine of psychic determinism and the view that human behavior is completely fixed after the early years of childhood, contained the seeds of a very different view. As Freud's pan-sexualism gave way to Jung's religious-philosophical approach, psychic determinism became psychic karma, a limited determinism which could be transcended. The Freudian concept of sublimation changed in connotation from that of a neurotic defense mechanism to the basic evolutionary impulse of Jungian analysis. Ideologies crumbled as lower, more restricted forms of behavior were viewed to give way to emergent, qualitatively higher modes of mental functioning. Where for Freud, society was the great frustrater of basic needs, with Jung, Adler, and others it became the great emancipator, leading the human animal from a primeval state of semiconsciousness through self-consciousness to the heights of altruism. Similarly, for Freud the mystic was the sick soul. The tortured ecstasies of the adept were to be viewed as the ultimate form of displacement wherein copious amounts of frustrated sexual energy find venue in neurotic mystical reverie. For Jung, however, this manner of sublimation represented the essence of the evolutionary impulse. It is with Jung that quasireligious humanism finds it greatest exponent.

Perhaps the most striking similarity of Jungian psychology to the view of the esoteric tradition can be found in his distinction between ego and self. For Jung, the ego is simply the moment-to-moment awareness of thoughts, feelings, perceptions, and intentions. It is Hume's "bundle of perceptions" and James's "empirical ego." In other words, it is the empiricist's notion of self; not some transcendent subject, but the everyday awareness of the individual.

The self, on the other hand, is a more obscure notion, and Jung was not entirely helpful in dispelling the uncertainty. In his earlier writings, he considered the self equivalent to the total personality, conscious and unconscious. But as his thought developed, he became convinced that there was, at the center of all human personality, a drive for unification, an imperative to be truly whole:

> If we picture the conscious mind with the ego as its center, as opposed to the unconscious, and if we now add to our mental picture the process of assimilating the unconscious, we can think of this assimilation as a kind of approximation of the conscious and unconscious, where the center of the total personality no longer coincides with the ego, but with a point midway between the conscious and unconscious. This would be the point of a new equilibrium, a new centering of the personality, a virtual center which, on account of its focal position between conscious and unconscious, ensures for the personality a new and more solid foundation (Hall 1957, 87-88).

The self is life's goal and is biographically represented in modern thought by the lives of Christ and the Buddha.

According to Jung, the self can develop only when all parts of the personality become fully developed and differentiated. Thus such sub-selves as the conscious and unconscious mind, the shadow and the persona, the anima and the animus must be brought out. Further, all of these diametrically opposed components must be synthesized into a harmonious whole. This unification can occur only with the aid of the "transcendent function," the intrapsychic process that synthesizes the dynamically opposed personality components. The transcendent function arises to bring about "the realization, in all of its aspects, of the personality originally hidden away in the embryonic germplasm, the production and unfolding of the original potential wholeness" (Hall 1957, 101).

Many commentators have placed Jung's rediscovery of the self at the top of the list of his accomplishments. Though many have taken the self to be basically spiritual in nature, and while Jung himself had remarked that religious experience is one of the closest approximations to realization of the self, the words "spiritual" and "religious" must be used guardedly here. It would be spurious to equate the self with the soul. Jung has laid the groundwork for a psychology somewhere between the theoretical extremes of reductionistic positivism and traditional theology. He made no commitment to the self's being an immortal entity. At the same time it is not an empirically observed thing, if by "empirical" we mean that which can be observed by the average person. But if there is indeed a mode of awareness that transcends that of the everyday manner of functioning, it may be possible to equate this with Jung's "self."

It is still important to note that the self as construed by Jung is to be distinguished from the more primal, metaphysical conception of the Self in the Vedas, as well as in other more patently mystical literature. Compare the previous passage from Jung with the following from the writings of the twentieth-century mystic Franklin Merrell-Wolff:

> While both subjective and objective factors are blended in Absolute Consciousness, yet the unitary quality is carried in the subjective moment. There is but one "I" or subject. Again this is the most immediate or intimate of all facts. Hence, only through the "I" is identity realized. Approached in any other way, God is ever something other than the seeker and, therefore, is at a distance. To come to the Father is to be at one with the Father, and this can be achieved only through the pure subject or SELF (Merrell-Wolff 1973a, 19).

At other points Merrell-Wolff talks about the transcendental consciousness, of which personal consciousness is part, which literally "sustains" the world. Regardless of the metaphysical judgments made of such an assertion, it is clear that the types of experiences described by the mystic are of a more radical nature than Jung's notion of a point halfway between the conscious and unconscious parts of the personality.

Even Jung's relatively limited concept of self, however, makes considerable inroads toward a transrational notion of personality. Jung's clients consisted generally of wealthy middle-aged men who had climbed the social and economic ladders and reached the top, only to find that even with success life was profoundly empty. Their lack of fulfillment set the stage for a new topic for psychological investigation. Jung's finding that all his patients suffered basically from a lack of meaning in life brought him to realize that people's answers to the existential questions indicate the condition of their psychological health. From these concerns emerged his view of the self.

Jung's concept of the equilibrium of selfhood set a precedent which became the basis for an original intellectual lineage in Western science. His notion of self, while avoiding the supernaturalism of the soul, put forth three tenets: 1) There is a greater psychological potential for humankind, and the optimum level of psycho-spiritual functioning has yet to be achieved by most people. 2) The actualization of this innate potential, which is tantamount to what he terms the realization of selfhood, is possible. 3) Selfhood is achieved by the unification of disparate parts of the personality. It was exactly these premises that laid the groundwork for humanistic psychology.

There have been a number of great humanistic thinkers in the past fifty years who have concentrated on the so-called "existential maroonment" of man and his chances for transcending the current psychological malaise. From psychology, Erich Fromm, Ronald Laing, and Victor Frankl are perhaps the best known. From philosophy, Sartre and Camus come to mind first. The views of these men range from social determinism to rugged individualism, and from radical optimism to a cautious, though hopeful, realism. But perhaps the greatest humanistic thinker of the past three decades and the man who will be most important for purposes of this book is Abraham H. Maslow.

The three most progressive elements of Maslow's psychology are his studies of peak experiences, self-actualizing people, and his theory of the hierarchical structure of needs. All of these will prove fundamental to the emerging conception of man being put forth here.

If it can be said that psychoanalysis has limited itself to the study of the psychologically sick, and behaviorism has been concerned with the "normal" or average man, then the work of Maslow has made humanism known for being concerned with the truly healthy, actualized, fulfilled individual. Maslow held that less than one percent of the population obtains self-actualization. This state is seen as the apex of individual fulfillment wherein all lower, subordinate, or antecedently necessary need-states have been fulfilled. On the face of it, actualization is the result of satisfying man's basic nature, a nature which is intrinsically good. All psychopathology, according to Maslow, is the result of the frustration of our innermost being. Maslow studied the lives of a number of subjects, living and dead, to ascertain the characteristics of the actualized individual. From his investigation of people like Lincoln, Jefferson, Walt Whitman, Henry Thoreau, Einstein, Eleanor Roosevelt, and Albert Schweitzer he amassed the following compendium of traits.

Actualized persons are 1) realistically oriented, 2) accept themselves, others and the world as they are, 3) spontaneous, 4) problem-centered rather than self-centered. 5) They have an air of emotional detachment and a need for privacy, 6) are autonomous and independent, 7) appreciative of people and the world in a fresh, rather than stereotyped way. 8) Most have had profound mystical or spiritual experience, though not necessarily religious in nature. 9) They identify with mankind, 10) and their relationships with a few people are profound, deeply emotional, and not superficial. 11) They have a democratic personality structure—for them all people are equal, 12) do not confuse means with ends, 13) and have a sense of humor that is philosophical, detached, but not hostile. 14) They are very creative, 15) resist conformity to culture, and 16) transcend, rather than merely cope with, the environment (Hall 1957, 328).

Once the lower needs are fulfilled (physical well-being, safety, love and belongingness, and esteem), no small undertaking in itself, there are eight ways to bring about actualization:

1) To experience everything fully and unself-consciously.
2) To make growth choices, as opposed to defense choices.
3) To follow the "inner voice," not some socially imposed or internalized standard.
4) To take responsibility for one's actions.
5) To know what one really prefers, and be honest about it.
6) To be the best one can at something.
7) To appreciate one's peak experiences.
8) To find out who one is, and what one would like to be (Maslow 1971, 41-53).

Maslow's conception of the self-actualized person does not contain any mystical element or a permanent "shift in consciousness" (peak experiences are temporary), yet it does seem in many ways to embody the notion of the altruistic, fully functioning, self-divested individual. This is the person who has combined a moral and intellectual autonomy with a naturalism that has transcended hedonistic self-consciousness. Maslow has written:

> Self-actualizing people are, without one single exception, involved in a cause outside their own skin, in something outside of themselves. . . . They are working at something which fate has called them to somehow, and which they work at and which they love, so that the work/joy dichotomy in them disappears (Maslow 1971, 43).

As stated earlier, Maslow constructed a hierarchy of needs, all of which must be fulfilled to achieve actualization. His view holds that: 1) Lower needs must be fulfilled before one can approach higher levels of need fixation; 2) no level can be omitted, skipped or gotten around; and 3) once a need is fulfilled, one is literally thrust without choice upon the next level of need fixation. This concept of need is significant both in that it holds psychological needs to be as real as physical ones, and that once a given level of need is satisfied one is forced to deal with the next level. There is thus a compelling natural imperative toward self-fulfillment. This view will be particularly significant throughout this book when I put forth the thesis that existential despair twentieth-century style is nothing less than our ascent from the level of material satisfaction, which the West has been largely successful in satisfying, to that of psychological fulfillment.

Spiritual Development and the Experience of Pure Consciousness

The groundwork has been laid for a broadly naturalistic view of man in which his ascent is seen as a gradual evolutionary progression through numerous hierarchically structured stages. Though evolution is not limited to the strictly physical realm—as "physical" has traditionally been defined—it is nonetheless a slow, cumulative process, rather than the foreordained craftwork of a personal Artisan. In accordance with this view, the individual man is not an immortal soul but a very complex system of hierarchically arranged, qualitatively different properties and processes commonly called "body and mind." The physical, chemical, biological, psychological, and spiritual functions are different levels that roughly correspond with physical and mental events. These levels of functioning are not all reducible to the lowest common denominator of physical laws. Instead there is an ontological as well as causal emergence: each progressive level of evolution may affect other more fundamental levels, as when psychological events bring about physical changes. Further, each level may be the grounding in which yet another higher set of properties and processes emerge. Such a naturalistic philosophy may countenance a grander view of man than has been the case with reductionism.

It should be pointed out that the "soul theory" and the evidence for pure consciousness do not rise and fall together. In fact, pure awareness has been directly experienced by a great many people. Many of the accounts from various mystics, sages, and philosophers center around such experiences. What exactly is pure consciousness? The Western philosopher W.T. Stace, in his work *Mysticism and Philosophy,* describes this state:

> Suppose that, after having got rid of all sensations, one should go on to exclude from consciousness all sensuous images, and then all abstract thoughts, reasoning processes, volitions, and other particular mental contents; what would then be left of consciousness? There would be no mental content whatsoever, but rather, a complete emptiness, vacuum, void. One would suppose *a priori* that consciousness would then entirely lapse and one would fall asleep or become

> unconscious. But the introvertive mystics—thousands of them all over the world—unanimously assert that they have attained to this complete vacuum of particular mental contents, but that what then happens is quite different from a lapse into unconsciousness. On the contrary, what emerges is a state of *pure* consciousness—"pure" in the sense that it is not the consciousness of any empirical content. It has no content except itself (Stace 1960, 85-86).

This is the "Unity of Apperception" of Kant. It is the very real state, experienced by yogis and adepts of the East, that was mistaken for the immortal, propertyless purusha. It is that profound state around which the world's greatest metaphysical systems have been built. An analogy is the blank movie screen after the film roll (of everyday consciousness) has run out. It is the undoing of all Western philosophical systems (such as that of Franz Brentano) that assert that all acts of consciousness must have an intentional object—a content (Aquila 1977, 1-25). Pure consciousness is introspective awareness that has run out of objects, but remains alert and empty. It is being conscious without being conscious *of* something.

Pure awareness is arrived at by increasingly refining introspective awareness until no empirical content remains. This state can be arrived at by a number of meditative techniques. Its benefits, as well as those of states that approximate it, are claimed to be many. Not only does the subject experience a moment of deep peace accompanied by great joy and vibrance at the actual time of realization, but there are pronounced after-effects. Some practitioners report greater energy throughout the day, a greater resistance to stress, depression, and fatigue, increased motivation, greater creativity, and even an increase in the ability to concentrate (Campbell 1974, 45-5). Furthermore, there are ever-increasing reports that the long-term effects of such experiences include augmented intellectual capacity, moral strength, and social concern.

Albert Einstein once said, "All religions, arts and

sciences are branches of the same tree." This is precisely the view of the enlightened society. Experiences of pure awareness, cultivated by the citizen of the new age, will be as much the object of the religious imperative as it will be the subject of scientific investigation. Not only would academic psychology benefit from the study of such states, but the everyday psychological health of the ordinary person would be greatly enhanced by working toward them as well. If even just part of the recent evidence concerned with meditative states is valid, the psychological, sociological, and religious impact of its widespread practice would be profound. Science, religion, and the arts would find a common pursuit and object of study, while society is transformed in the process.

There are reports from all sides that the current "average man" is lacking something. It is my contention that meditative experiences such as those just discussed may help provide the missing piece of the puzzle. The eighteenth-century enlightenment from which the benefits of secular science and a high standard of (material) living arose must be supplemented by a twenty-first century enlightenment. This second version will cultivate various psycho-spiritual techniques with the aim of fulfilling man's total nature, not just his material needs.

What Is Enlightenment?

The topic of enlightenment is so wide, so pervasive, and so all-encompassing that I must admit the following discussion will not do it justice. Perhaps no other topic in the philosophy of religion has been the arena for such a wide variety of related issues, all of which must be adequately dealt with to study the notion of enlightenment satisfactorily. Further, the great disparity of theory, practice, and achieved ends with respect to the state of enlightenment makes any comprehensive investigation necessarily encyclopedic.

This disparity is evident in the literature of mysticism and philosophy of various different schools, East and West. The very names given to the blessed states suggest a plethora of possibilities. From Zen we hear of *satori,* while yogic literature talks of *dhyana* and *samadhi.* Vedanta talks of Unity consciousness and God consciousness, while the Buddhist faithfully prods onward to his nirvana. Modern Western mysticism has adopted the term "cosmic consciousness," while various other schools use a spectrum of terms, many of which carry orthodox religious connotations. "Union with God," "blessedness," and "salvation" are examples. Conversely, nonreligious, secular, and atheistic orientations provide a sundry list of religiously neutral words such as "the Recognition," or "the Transition." Some of these terms are said to be coextensive with the state of enlightenment, while others hold that enlightenment is a prelude to, or the culminating stage of, the particular state in question. For example, it is said that the Buddha attained enlightenment long before he entered nirvana.

The most obvious questions at this point are whether or not all of these names are different terms for the same state, and if not, how they are related. The first question is more readily answered than the second. It is obvious from the literature to even the most perfunctory of researchers that, at best, all of the above form a wide spectrum of possible paranormal psychological states. Each term serves to designate different levels, types, or aspects of the generic state called "enlightenment." The school of thought one adheres to, as well as the various practices one follows, may have the greatest impact on the eventual state achieved. For example, the description of Zen *satori* and that of yogic *samadhi* are highly disparate. The former is marked by a freshness of perception so acute that it obliterates the usual way of looking at the world through a wall of thought and memory. All is seen as if for the first time. *Samadhi,* on the other hand, appears to be a highly introverted state wherein the subject has lost track of all objects, external and internal, except for pure awareness itself. The desired ends of different traditions, then, are quite distinct; consequently, the aspirant should choose a path in accordance with his desired goal. What we term "enlightenment" designates a broad continuum of psychological states, varying in degree of intensity and marked by differing phenomenal experiences and behavioral results.

Additionally, the ways to enlightenment vary from school to school and temperament to temperament. As just one example, the Hindu tradition alone advocates four different possible paths: *bhakti yoga, raja yoga, jnana yoga,* and *karma yoga.* These are the ways of devotion, experience, knowledge, and work or duty, respectively. The first path emphasizes devotion to a personal God while the latter three stress self-salvation to one degree or another. Further, within each path there is a plethora of possible different combinations of practices, forms of meditation, and life-regimens.

Finally, the utter plurality respective to this topic is not limited to possible end states and to paths *to* these states. As might be expected, the accompanying metaphysical doctrines accompanying different approaches are at least as diverse. Some schools such as *samkhya yoga* emphasize the necessity of belief in a personal God, while Buddhist doctrine, at least in its original form, completely divorces itself from such concerns, moving to a religious agnosticism if not outright atheism. Similarly, whether there is, at bottom, an immortal soul is of controversy. While most schools of Indian philosophy accept the existence of the soul in one form or another, original Buddhism does not.

Two final matters of controversy are the relationship of mystical experiences to the quest, and the aspirant's attitude toward the goal of enlightenment. Regarding the first, some literature, particularly associated with the Vedas, seems to suggest that enlightenment is something like a permanent mystical state or at least the point from which one may enter such a state at will. Other schools seem to minimize the connection between overt mysticism and the very practical matter of personal development. Already so much has been written on this issue that to attempt a recapitulation here would be futile and presumptuous. But even a cursory glance at the literature reveals the distance between different perspectives on this point.

The last controversial point to be addressed concerns the seeker's attitude toward his desired end. Put simply, should the aspirant *want*, or make the search for enlightenment as an *object* of fulfillment. To do so seems contrary to the very philosophy of the East, which stresses freedom from desire, even this most important of desires. The student is admonished to work hard, to prepare, and to take every precaution to further his spiritual development, but not to *try* for enlightenment. Just as a watched pot never boils, so the aspirant must discipline himself in an unself-conscious manner. There is another view on the issue, however, embodied in the following tale:

A master and his student are floating downstream in a boat, talking of spiritual matters. At one point the student asks the master, "How hard must I want enlightenment to achieve it?"

The master responds by throwing the student overboard and purposely holding the neophyte's head beneath the water for a long moment. Finally the teacher relents and pulls the student back out of the water. "How hard did you want the air?" asks the master.

"With all of my being," answers the student.

"Well, you must want enlightenment more."

It is obvious from the above discussion that those who are supposedly actualized, realized, or enlightened differ and contradict one another as to theories and contentions about ultimate reality. For example some believe in a psychological center of the personality while others do not. This is true for questions like that of God, of the personal afterlife, of whether there is a heaven or a hell. The atheist and the theist cannot both be right; one of the groups must be wrong. Who are we to believe, and more importantly, what good is this state if it still leads to uncertainty on the most pressing metaphysical issues that confront man?

This question strikes to the heart of a number of epistemological issues. The lay reader is confounded and perplexed with the mystical contention that all apparently separate things are a unity, and that all of reality is basically mental in nature. And though I have expressly avoided the metaphysical problems of idealism versus realism, the epistemological problem remains just the same: what is this enlightenment if it cannot help clear up the most significant issues of all time?

The answer to be put forward here will not please the dogmatic on any side. Basically, it must be that although spiritual progress is a reality and has great moral, psychological, and social import, it is not a "hot line" to Ultimate Reality. Believing something does not make it true. Despite the contentions of some mystics, wrapped in their beatific visions or rocked gently in the arms of some relative of Morpheus, the assurance that pain is illusory, for example, holds little consolation for the poor, the sick, and the dying. Likewise with similar assertions. In short, spiritual development fosters psychological equanimity, but not epistemological certitude.

I must echo the Buddhist parable of the man who has been wounded by an arrow. A surgeon arrives at the scene to save the patient, but he will not allow the arrow to be removed until he knows who shot him, where this man comes from, what material the bow and arrow are constructed of, etc. Before finding all of this out, the man would be dead:

> Similarly it is not on the view that the world is eternal, that it is finite, that body and soul are distinct, or that the Buddha exists after death that a religious life depends. Whether these views or the opposite are held . . . there is still old age, there is death, and grief, lamentation, suffering, sorrow and despair. . . . I have not spoken of these views because they do not conduce to absence of passion, tranquility, and Nirvana (Smith 1958, 106).

What is most important is development—not metaphysics.

With respect to the validity of the mystical experience, William James makes three points:

1) Mystical states, when well developed, usually are, and have the right to be, absolutely authoritative over the individual to whom they come.
2) No authority emanates from them which should make it a duty for those who stand outside of them to accept their revelations uncritically.
3) They break down the authority of the non-mystical or rationalistic consciousness, based upon the understanding and the senses alone. They show it to be only one kind of consciousness. They open out the possibility of other orders of truth, in which, so far as anything in us vitally responds to them, we may freely continue to have faith (James 1961, 331).

James, in his cautious open-mindedness, seems to have said it best.

It has recently been argued by psychologist Charles Tart that certain states of consciousness may have an empirical value superior in some ways to other such states (Tart 1980, 200-212). But to avoid falling head first into reckless idealism, I must maintain that whatever empirical import such states have is ultimately subjective. While no one would doubt the intensity and even overwhelming nature of mystical experiences, and that the individual may be permanently psychologically transformed by such experiences, still it would take strong evidence to show that such interludes lead to insights about the objective world.

So much for the variety of issues related to the notion of enlightenment. It is time to address the most central issues: What is it? Is it constituted, as some have argued, by a "shift in consciousness"? Is there really a state beyond the everyday subject/object awareness? Or is it, as many have argued, a carefully cultivated form of pathology?

Before commencing this enquiry, we must be reminded

that insofar as many distinct states fall under the rubric of "enlightenment," what might apply to one particular state does not necessarily pertain to another. For example, M.N. Roy has argued that the state known as *samadhi* is a form of self-induced mental coma (Roy 1950, 53-102). Far from being superhuman, it is subhuman; far from being spiritually or psychologically beneficial, it may be quite dangerous. Whether or not this accusation is valid, this statement cannot be generalized to other types of states such as *satori*. Thus each particular state must be examined individually, without regard for the determination with respect to other states.

A second important point to clarify is that actualization should not be confused with enlightenment. Psychological characteristics such as "democratic personality structure," "very spontaneous," and "very creative" may be thought of as the direction in which one wants to develop. While both the actualized and the enlightened exhibit such characteristics, the enlightened personality seems to manifest them to a greater extreme than the actualized personality. For example, a democratic personality structure means being equally disposed to all other individuals so that the rights accorded to one would be accorded to all. The actualized person looks beyond roles, castes, race, religion, or sex. The right to life, for example, transcends smaller utilitarian concerns. But whereas the actualized person might extend this principle to all humanity, the enlightened one goes further still, extending his protective aegis to all animals. Thus the literature of the Orient is replete with examples of the doctrine of nonviolence extended to even the smallest insect. The practicality of such measures is not the point. What is important is that the sense of moral duty is so pervasive in the enlightened individual that he follows through on such conduct as a matter of course. This applies to the other personality traits as well.

Beyond this, however, there is something more, something wholly "other" about the enlightened personality. The wisdom, charm, and moral compassion of such a person strikes one, time and again, as that of the deity. It is little wonder that the Buddha and Christ, both undoubtedly enlightened, were deified by their followers after their deaths. Thus the enlightened personality takes on a form so radically different from that of the everyday psychological predisposition toward the world that great religious and philosophical movements coalesce around it.

What is it that fundamentally characterizes the enlightened personality? From all of the literature on the subject, ancient and modern, it appears that there is a shift, in all of the various states described as enlightenment, in the perceived division of the world between subject and object. This is in contrast with everyday awareness by which the world is divided between the "me," the subject, and the "not me," or object. The subject is all with which I am most intimately concerned and by which I *identify* myself. It could probably be meaningfully argued that the distinction between subject and object is marked by a continuum of gradations from subject to object, rather than an abrupt dichotomy. For example, there is certainly a given amount of self-identification I entertain in my possession of certain objects (see Chapter Four, "Having Man"). I feel violated, in a sense, if my house is broken into. Still, one does not usually consider tangible belongings as *part* of oneself in any significant way. On the other hand, if my hand were to be amputated, I would surely consider this to have an effect on a basic part of *me*. Even this would not be as intrusive, however, as if I learned I would have to undergo psychosurgery to change my personality. My personality is somehow more me than even my hand. Thus, the subject shades off into object in everyday consciousness.

To the enlightened person, however, this dichotomy has ceased to be meaningful. There simply appears to be no significant distinction between self and object, in a psychological sense. This is not to say that such a person fails to interact as a discrete physical entity in the world. He nourishes himself and moves from harm's way, for example. Subject and object are obliterated in a different sense, however. The enlightened personality comes to perceive all of those attributes that ordinary people see as "personal" as external to his basic self. His body, his memories, his intellectual capacities, his possessions are all as "other" to the basic self, as though they belonged to another person. From his point of view, everything about one except the pure self, as represented in pure consciousness, is contingent, accidental, unimportant.

Interestingly, the literature on the subject has described this process in two seemingly contradictory ways. Some have perceived enlightenment as the disappearance of the ego, the obliteration of the subject of everyday awareness. For this group, everything in the world is equally objective. My capacities and experiences are as objective or external to me as are your capacities, experiences and possessions. Nothing distinguishes "me" from "you" because both are equally objective, contingent, and accidental.

The second group views the state of enlightenment as an expansion of the subject to include the object. When all of your properties, capacities, and possessions become as important as mine, there is no longer any meaningful reason to attribute a greater subjectiveness to my intelligence, or my kindness, or my physical characteristics than to yours. All are equally important.

These descriptions are complementary ways of describing one basic principle: for the enlightened personality, the dichotomy between subject and object loses its meaning. The practical import of this may be summarized in the following three principles, each of which represents this same process from differing perspectives:

1) There is a change in the individual's self-concept that approximates an expanded sense of selfhood.
2) There is a change in the individual's concept of the other such that all but the "pure self" is perceived as objective, external, and contingent.
3) There is a change in the relation *between* self and

other, in accordance with the first two changes, such that the self takes greater responsibility for, has greater sympathy for, and acts in greater respect of the other.

The first of these three principles may be best presented by analogy. Richard M. Bucke has argued that just as the difference between the animal's "simple consciousness" and human self-consciousness involves an expansion in self-consciousness, similarly there is a parallel expansion in the shift from self-consciousness to what he calls "cosmic consciousness" (Bucke 1901, 62-87). Thus, the animal has no conception whatsoever of itself as a being apart from the world at large. It certainly acts to preserve itself, defends its territory, and in all usual respects acts as an autonomous agent; still, it probably does not conceive of itself as an independent entity in contrast with the world in the same way that persons do. It has no sense of selfhood.

Thus, the transition to a greater sense of self as embodied in the notion of enlightenment means that the subject learns to treat as sacred, even as primary, more than his own being—to include that which is other. This expansion of selfhood manifests in a number of ways: in a greater compassion for others; in an exalted moral sense which demands political and social equality for all; or in the more metaphysical or religious feeling that "thou art that," the literal extension of self-being to include all of the universe. The subjective feeling of transcendence of all apparent plurality into the absolutely idealistic One amounts to the most extreme version of a process that may manifest itself in a variety of ways.

The obverse side of the coin is found in the second principle. The psychological state of enlightenment is characterized by a de-emphasis of those qualities considered central to the personality by the unenlightened. Physical and mental attributes, accidents of birth resulting in social class, eventual level of education, and other fortuitous circumstances are seen for the accidental and contingent properties of the individual which they are. As a result, there is an elimination of ego identification with these things.

The third principle, or the shift in the relationship between subject and object, self and other, is characterized by a greater level of harmonious interdependence or what has been called "synergy" by some. On the social level, this is manifest by the cooperative interaction of disparate groups and individuals; on the international level by peaceful coexistence among nations; and on the natural level by the rewards for having understood, rather than ignored, the laws of nature.

The truly enlightened person then, is neither a renunciate nor a hermit. Instead, he combines the discipline of the *sadhu* with the worldliness of the modern cosmopolitan, the individuality of a Thoreau with the sociopolitical awareness of an Aristotle, the serene equanimity of a Lao Tzu with the drive and motivation of a Winston Churchill. He faithfully strives to combine what Nietzsche called the "Dionysion" (spontaneous primal energy) with the "Apollonian" (ordered, rational force). He is the great synthesizer and brings the true goal of life back to earth. He is all that the great minds, East and West, have admired.

In these first two chapters, I have attempted to address a number of the most fundamental questions important to man. These questions and their corresponding answers must be considered prior to all value judgments. In other words, before we can know what the good life is and how to implement it, we must know our own nature. Questions of mind and matter, substance and process, freedom and determinism should not be disregarded, relegated to the realm of pin-dancing angels as so many seem to think. Instead, they are the most important questions to ask because only when they have been answered can we make intelligent value and policy choices. As Roger Sperry has written:

> Doctrine regarding ultimate values is closely tied to beliefs about the properties of the human psyche or conscious mind and its relation to physical reality. . . . So long as the nature of mind and the mind-body

> relation remained shrouded in mystery, the spectrum of possibilities was almost unlimited; the whole problem of human values floated in a wide open sea of uncertainty where science could hardly get started, and value belief systems of necessity had to be built on conjecture, intuition and revelation (Sperry 1983, 2).

This investigation of the nature of man so necessarily preceded an investigation of the individual and society where these doctrines are applied and the corresponding values implemented. If these first chapters constitute a philosophy of man, the next four will develop a general psychology of man—both as he is and as he could be. At the farthest reaches of human nature, man the mystic, the scientist, and the social engineer will be fused and will be the living exemplar of the enlightened society.

II

Evolution and Enlightenment

3

The Evolution of Consciousness: Three Axes of Psychological Development

If the position outlined to this point could be summed up in a few words, it would be that of naturalism without reductionism. Life is a product of the gradual progress of nature, but life is not fully understood simply by appealing to the laws of physics. Nature is progressive, not only in the sense that larger and larger buildings are built out of the same old stones, but in the sense that altogether novel types of "building blocks" emerge as the evolutionary process continues. This is evolution at the most general level, embracing everything from the physical to the psycho-spiritual.

If evolution occurs in an emergent fashion at the biological and cosmic levels, as has been elaborated here, then it is not implausible that a similar process should be taking place at the individual psychological level as well. As matter emerged from energy roughly 100,000 years after the Big Bang, so mind emerged from matter billions of years later. And, as evolution is not simply a transordinal process (a process that "bridges" the different levels, e.g., energy-to-matter or matter-to-mind) but may also occur on a single level (from one type of animal life to another, for example), so evolution on the level of the psychological seems quite likely. For example, new systems of needs, beliefs, values, and behavioral dispositions may replace similar previous systems. Psychological, moral, and spiritual evolution could proceed in this manner. Though psycho-spiritual evolution may sometimes occur spontaneously and at other times only with deliberate effort, that such a process occurs cannot be gainsaid. Both Western developmental psychology and Eastern mysticism share this commitment, though the theories by which each school of thought explains human development differ.

I am not unmindful of the fact that it is notoriously difficult to erect a theory of psychology on a foundation of metaphysical commitments. The gulf between cosmology and psychology is well littered with the far-flung fragments of crossing bridges attempted by philosophers, ancient and modern. Well apprised of the difficulties, I will use the metaphysical as a point of departure, a suggestion or intimation of the natural psychological process. If nature works by a process of evolution, and if this process operates in an emergent fashion, then it seems quite plausible that this same process can be readily measured and observed on the highest level of development in the history of the universe to date—the psychological level of man. While evolution may still be operating physically or chemically at this time, its main thrust has moved to the mental level. Self-conscious intention may, like a wheel, carry along all of the lower-level processes within the system's structure as it rolls along to a greater destination.

In the following chapters three main tenets will be put forward. First, the process of evolution is continuing on at the psycho-spiritual level in man. It operates in a fashion similar to that of physical evolution, by lawful emergence of new need/value orientation, psychologically distinct from previous need/value systems but causally interactive with and dependent on these other systems. (Thus, Freud's contention that the spiritual drive has its origin in the forces of the libido may be true, though his claim that the spiritual quest is the result of a frustrated sexual drive is rejected. Rather, the healthy personality may derive spiritual energy from the more fundamental sexual impulse, but this spiritual impulse can only arise when the more basic need is satisfied or transcended. In other words, the spiritually advanced is the sexually-satisfied, not frustrated, individual. In this manner, the "higher" need may emerge from the lower need, but is distinct from it.) One last implication of this first principle is that psychological evolution is superior to physical evolution in the sense that it is more efficient. Thousands of generations of evolution might be required to effect a physical change that could be accomplished in a single life, with a simple readjustment of behavior on the part of the individual. It is this psychological development that makes behavioral adaptability more efficient.

The second tenet put forth in the chapters to come is that what is commonly experienced as the religious or psycho-spiritual need in modern man is itself a high-level emergent need with its own particular evolutionary impact (see Chapter Ten). The continued failure of our culture to understand the nature of this need and its true function is the genesis of a great portion of modern social-psychological turmoil.

The third tenet holds that what has been termed the "psycho-spiritual" need does have a proper means of satisfaction; further, it is possible to measure development which accompanies its satisfaction. In this chapter, three general criteria for assessing this development in the individual and society as a whole will be put forth. "Psycho-spiritual" development—the term I have used to designate a wide class of psychological, moral, and spiritual needs and predispositions in man—will be measured in an individual: 1) by the level of need fixation; 2) by the level of self-identification; and 3) by the types of things or experiences in which an individual characteristically finds meaning and happiness.

It is evident in everyday life that different individuals are moved and motivated by different things, see themselves in different ways, and take pleasure in different activities, pursuits, possessions, and lifestyles. It is equally clear that any particular individual is capable of changing his preferences and needs. But what is sometimes debated is whether the individual who changes does so in a principled or ordered manner, by determined or determinable routes. It is exactly this point that is at the basis of modern developmental psychology. From Maslow to Erikson and others, lawlike schemes and hierarchies of human development are seen as at the root of developmental theory. As recently put: "Further, studies made by developmental psychologists indicate that change is not random; it progresses step by step from relatively simple, immature states toward more complex, wide-ranging, more balanced states. Human growth can be thought of as an ordered sequence—a hierarchy—advancing in response to changing drives from the undeveloped toward the developed" (Mitchell 1983, 3).

Having, Doing, Being

This principle, as elaborated by Arnold Mitchell, Director of the Stanford Research Institute Values and Lifestyle Program, is borne out in the course of research reported in *The Nine American Lifestyles.* In this work, Mitchell distinguishes what he calls Survivors, Sustainers, Belongers, Emulators, Achievers, I-Am-Me's, Experientials, the Societally Conscious, and the Integrateds. Mitchell's scheme is but one of a number of similar progressive hierarchies. Those of Maslow, Fromm, and Erikson divide the categories differently, but there is an incredible similarity in the characterization of the various types of lifestyles and personalities and in the congruity in the order of the sequence. In the next few chapters, I will present a similar developmental hierarchy, though simpler than many of the established theories. By contrast, this theory introduces only three modes of self-development, designated as Having man, Doing man, and Being man. Because there are fewer categories, a wider range of personality and behavior will be subsumed under any one classification in this model, as compared with other schemes. For example, Having man seems roughly coextensive with Survivors, Sustainers, and to lesser degree Belongers, Emulators, and Achievers in Mitchell's scheme.

Besides the simplicity of our Having-Doing-Being trichotomy, my view differs from traditional developmental schemes in another important way. The hierarchy outlined here examines the realm of human psychological development beyond what is generally acknowledged by modern Western psychology. Self-realized Doing man, the second of the three categories in order of development, embraces the most advanced level recognized in Western psychology. The stage of Doing man at its highest reaches is similar to Mitchell's Integrated stage or Maslow's self-actualized individual. But even a higher level of individual psycho-spiritual achievement is possible, embodied in the image of Being man. Being man is the enlightened soul of Oriental and esoteric literature. And though Being man is a rare creature in our world, nonetheless the possibility for this level of development is real.

Before moving on, I must state clearly that the Having-Doing-Being trichotomy is not the result of any in-depth scientific analysis on my part. I have conducted no empirical investigation to determine the applicability of wide psychological constructs or labels for more specific dimensions of personality. I believe much of this work has already been done, and I draw openly and gratefully upon the work of others. Instead, Having man, Doing man, and Being man are intended as three simple but powerful images—metaphors for modes of human existence—delineated to capture what is most essential about three typically different orientations toward life. What is lost by lack of empirical precision is gained in simplicity and comprehensiveness. Further, though few individuals or societies, if any, are completely reducible to one type, I believe an overall pattern is discernible in any individual, or for that matter, in any particular culture. The way that one sees oneself and the way in which one finds meaning most reveals who one really is. Perhaps more importantly, the way one sees oneself and thereby finds a depth of meaning in living is most indicative of who one might become. Thus, what follows is as much vision as it is science, as much hope as it is theory, as prescriptive as it is descriptive. But humankind *is* the point at which all of these may be merged into one and the same. We are free to the extent that we can institute and guide the causes and influences that will shape our life and world. We are determined to the degree that we fail to do so.

Self-identification

One of the most interesting of psychological notions is that people *identify with* a variety of things that are basically external to their innermost selves, i.e., their own natural tendencies, abilities, and predispositions. But what exactly do we mean by "identify"?

The act of identification occurs when a conscious subject "reaches out" to an object—to something beyond itself—and attempts to possess, to control, or to see itself in this object. This phenomenon has been noted both in a variety of Eastern doctrines, including the work of Shankara, the yogic philosophers, and others, and in Western philosophy and psychology by such sundry thinkers as Sartre, R.D. Laing, and Gordon Allport. In *Being and Nothingness,* for example, the twentieth-century French existentialist Jean-Paul Sartre conducts an extended analysis of "bad faith," his term for the type of role-playing that occurs when an individual seeks to escape the freedom of the unattached self by adopting some external guise, strategy, or identity. The man who is unsure of himself in a romantic situation identifies with his more successful older brother. By doing so he relinquishes something of his own identity and "becomes" his brother. He thinks, speaks, and comports himself in a manner consistent with the way he perceives his brother to be. The scene is familiar in any social situation where an individual is observed to change, to distort, or to modify his behavior patterns to act in accord with the group.

This process of "taking on" another's identity in a cognitive-symbolic fashion is only one aspect of the process of identification. Typically, one identifies with something because the object is either overtly expedient or symbolically meaningful. Thus the diffident lover from the previous example and the primitive who sees himself in the power of the lion are both identifying with objects, though in different ways. Ultimately, however, all acts of identification are at bottom motivated by utilitarian concerns. The subject identifies because identification gives him something—power, meaning, a goal in life.

Identification is the assumption of a pattern, an experience, a lifestyle, or an object with some purpose in mind. The act of identification involves a preoccupation with the object. It infuses meaning and lends a purpose to existence, but it may also simultaneously prohibit an individual from following a course of action that would be more amenable or natural to his own constitution. Thus the artist who becomes a businessman may fall further and further away from his own natural predisposition, and this may have pernicious psychological effects (Maslow 1962).

It is evident that people may come to identify with an endless range of things: objects, experiences, hopes, people, power, profession, to name just a few. In the course of identification, the object not only indues one with some psychological meaning, but the individual may come to see the object as part of his essential self, building an entire life around it. For example, a person who strongly identifies with money not only exerts his entire being in its pursuit, but other aspects of his life may also revolve around the pursuit of money. Love may come to be subjugated to the demand for monetary accumulation, as an avaricious woman marries a wealthy man. To the power-seeking politician, the delight in public appearances may derive all of its energy from the knowledge that the more primary motive—power—is being furthered. Thus the personality may be seen as a hierarchy of primary, secondary, and less influential object identifications, with some of the less essential ones as outgrowths of the more primary.

A great deal has been written on the subject of identification—from Freud to Adler to the esoteric thinkers of the East. There is controversy as to whether the objects blind the self to its own true nature (Shankara) or, instead, may be a very meaningful basis for an otherwise vacuous personality (Sartre). More will be said about this in Chapter Six, but one fact has a consensus: identification does take place.

It is my contention that not only does identification occur, but the types of things with which an individual characteristically identifies may provide an insight into what type of personality he is. In short, what the individual identifies with provides an indication of who he is, what he values, and thus, what his particular level of psycho-spiritual advancement may be.

In the tripartite scheme of Having, Doing, and Being personalities, the Haver, at the lower level of human development, is the personality type that most readily and consummately identifies with objects and things—in short, the tangible. The relationship between the Having personality and the external world is best characterized as that of ownership. Such a person finds self-identification, psychological import, and existential meaning in the material things that he owns—the new car, the house, even the friends that he "possesses." Thus the Haver finds self-worth and literally sees him*self* reflected in the things that he owns. Thus, identification is a vitally important determinant in the behavior of the Having personality. The rigid identification of the Haver makes him the most psychologically unstable of the three types, while being the most predictable behaviorally.

The intermediate level of individual and social development is that of the Doing personality. The Doing man finds significance in experience. On the axis of self-identification, the Doing personality identifies with all that he has experienced—what his profession is, where he has traveled, what he has seen, whom he has loved. The nature of the relationship between such a person and the external world is that of experience, transience, and the conspicuous consumption of life-events. Where the Haver finds existential import in possession, the Doing personality has transcended the rather static tendency to hold onto things in a possessive manner. Rather than clinging to the constant, the Doing personality, at its lower reaches, wallows in the uncertainty of continuous movement from one experience to the next. It is this lack of continuity in self-identification, resulting from identifying with a long chain of experiences, that effects the so-called "identity crisis" in the Doing personality. He has no "center" of experience, no constant in which to anchor himself. The identity crisis is only one of a wide variety of problems and advantages endemic of the Doing stage, both at the individual level and as it affects society in general (see Chapter Five).

At the apex of this hierarchy is the Being personality. Being man, by far the least populous of our three stages, is characterized by a marked absence of existential dependence on external conditions and circumstances. The Being personality has learned to enjoy external things and experience without being psychologically dependent on them. Instead, such a person has found an inner source of grace and stability in the awareness that comes from a greater depth of self-knowledge. Being man will be examined in Chapter Six.

It should be noted that the level of self-identification can be measured at the social as well as the individual level. In the following chapters, the particular goals and institutions that a society endorses—along with the function such aspirations and institutions have in the social process—will be shown as important criteria for determining a society's level of psycho-spiritual progression.

Meaning

There is an old anecdote about a Harvard philosophy examination consisting of one word: Why? The respondents were said to receive an automatic failure if they embarked on a long philosophical foray into alternative analyses of the question. On the other hand, the "B" response, equally laconic to the question, was simply: Because. The best of all answers, however, and the only one to warrant the cherished Harvard "A," was, appropriately enough: Why not?

The great Why questions of philosophy have been subject to the unrelenting abuse of most twentieth-century philosophers. Heidegger has been roundly criticized as an obscurantist, and his "Why is there anything at all?" has become known as the paragon of meaningless questions. (Anything that serves to explain the rest of the universe and thus answer the "super-ultimate why" must itself have some explanation—and on ad infinitum.) What is the meaning of life? has earned the ubiquitous contempt of philosophers as diverse as existentialists and those of the analytic school. Still, there is a certain longing, a sincerity in the question of meaning, and no work concerned with the human situation can thoroughly dispose of the issue. For my part here, I will examine the notion of *subjective* meaning: What is meaningful for individuals?

There has been a great diversity of ways that man has justified his day-to-day existence down through the ages. These are attempts to order one's existence, to gain release, or to seek fulfillment and balance against the weight of the burden of life. These are the rewards of living, the elements of a lifestyle for which we are thankful. The question, What is the meaning of life? thus gets transposed into, How do different individuals typically find meaning?

Existentialist philosophers and third-wave psychologists have long struggled with the so-called "existential vacuum" characteristic of the present century. Some seek ultimate meaning in God, others in the quest for authenticity. Abraham Maslow, the late American humanistic psychologist, attempted to chart a new course in his writings, combining elements of naturalism with transpersonal psychology. He wrote:

> Without the transcendent and the transpersonal we get sick, violent and nihilistic, or else hopeless and apathetic. We need something greater than we are to be awed by and to commit ourselves to in a new, naturalistic, empirical, non-churchly sense, perhaps as Thoreau and Whitman, William James, and John Dewey did (Maslow 1962, 31).

In the final analysis, the search for meaning is in essence a search for what is most real about us as human beings. But a human is not a static creature. Rather, he exhibits a development, a progression of modes of the discovery of meaning in life. These modes are correlative to the three stages of Having, Doing, and Being.

At the most fundamental level, the Having stage is an indication of the struggle for survival and the need for the satisfaction of physical needs. The Having stage, however, includes not only those who are struggling to meet their most basic needs—those who do not yet *have* much of anything. It also includes those who have met those needs but continue to act as if they haven't, accumulating more than any one person needs to survive and to live a normal life. Meaning at the Having stage is more aligned with physical gratification and is not, strictly speaking, psycho-spiritual fulfillment at all.

It is only at the Doing level of personality that notions of the meaning of life begin to emerge, and may grow into a preoccupation. It is at this level that the individual strives to discover what he *is* beyond what he owns. Material possessions are de-emphasized as such a person attempts to find himself in what he *does*. Progression through the Doing level of the hierarchy is the most painful of times, as one has relinquished the sense of meaning found in possession while not yet arriving at a new pattern for organizing life. The "existential void" is characteristic of the transition from the Having to the Doing level of development. Meaning is endorsed as it is revealed in experience. Camus' "ethic of quantity" (of experience), which imputes a higher value on the quantity than the quality of experience, is endemic of this stage. More will be said in Chapter Five about a number of modern philosophies which have arisen in the twentieth century to address this issue.

The most stable level of meaning is found at the level of Being, the apex of our tripartite hierarchy. Meaning at this stage is no longer dependent on objects and experiences. The Being-level personality still enjoys worldly tastes and experiences, but may live a meaningful life without those things that are so psychologically important to others. Existence itself, for itself, is manifestly significant. The Being personality has transcended the hedonistic doctrine that the good, the bad, the sacred, and the profane may be measured by a calculus of pleasure and pain. It is not what occurs *in* existence but existence itself that indues such a person with an abiding sense of joy.

The three stages of meaning as summarily presented here should be seen as a continuum of experience. The great majority of those living in contemporary Western society incorporate elements of more than one level. Still it is possible to render a general classification of a given individual along the continuum by considering his predominant approach to life. Put simply, many individuals are generally oriented toward the level of Having or of Doing, each with minor elements of the other involved.

The Level of Need Fixation

A number of important things must be said about the nature of need in general before continuing on to the third general criterion for evaluating the level of psycho-spiritual development in individuals. The first concerns the theory of Abraham Maslow with respect to the concept of need. As already discussed, Maslow constructed and elaborated a hierarchy of needs based on his research on various subjects, both psychologically healthy and neurotic. Maslow's basic concept was that of "pre-potency," the notion that certain "lower" needs must be fulfilled before the subject becomes aware of higher level needs, and that once a need has been satisfied, the individual automatically and irretrievably reaches the next highest level of need confrontation. Even if we reject Maslow's particular ordering of needs—e.g., love needs must be satisfied before esteem and task competence needs are—the notion of prepotency is in itself a vital theoretical device, important as the psychological equivalent to emergent evolution. Further research may thus revise, modify, or extend the hierarchy of needs while still maintaining the central notion of prepotency.

A second important consideration is that the concept of need has, particularly in the West, been confined to what might be called "survival needs." Thus, food is a need, it has been argued, but the pursuit of love is only a luxury. One can survive without love; thus one does not *need* it. But this approach is unfortunate. Maslow, among others, distinguishes between growth and deficit needs (Maslow 1971). The latter are survival needs such as for food or water, while the former are psychological needs such as for artistic expression, social acceptance, or affection. Growth needs are as vital to full human functioning as are deficit or survival needs. It is obvious that all people, regardless of level of development, continue to require lower level need satisfaction. Everyone needs to eat, for example. It is simply that at a higher level, attention is not primarily fixed on this need.

There are three reasons for extending the concept of need to include the psycho-spiritual needs. First, the desire for love or self-expression presents itself as a genuine yearning, an imperative demanding attention.

The individual subjectively experiences the *need* to satisfy it. Second, a great deal of recent evidence indicates that failure to satisfy such needs may promote both physical and mental illnesses (Jourard 1977, 75-100). It is well documented that mental stress is directly related to as much as eighty to ninety percent of all illnesses (Russell 1976). The failure to find love, to express oneself, to engage in meaningful employment, or to curtail a period of grieving may result in illnesses from long-term chronic mental problems to abrupt and devastating physical disabilities. Maslow himself contended that the satisfaction of the need for love is as essential to continued good health as is Vitamin C.

Finally, the third argument for relegating such desires to the status of needs is that the satisfaction of such needs appears to stabilize the personality and place the subject one step closer to self-actualization. Satisfaction leads to improvement and development. Once satisfaction is achieved, the individual may enjoy the object of the need (e.g., social acceptance) from the vantage point of control and enjoyment, rather than fixation, aberration, and stagnation.

In accordance with the foregoing analysis, there are three general levels of need fixation correlative with the levels of Having, Doing, and Being. The continuum of development is marked by a general trend toward increasing independence from the environment. The Having level of need is marked by fixation at the level of physical need. In the environment where there is scarcity of resources, there is a constant fight for survival. Need at this level has an obvious evolutionary function. Man must eat to stay alive, and little else is important at this primitive stage. But even though he begins to consolidate his power, as the satisfaction of physical needs becomes easier with the growth of society, of technology, and of more effective means of distribution, man remains oriented to physical ownership. Thus the role of the Haver in modern society is that of the hoarder, the exploiter, and the imperialist.

With the transition to the level of Doing, man begins to recognize and to suffer under the weight of a new set of needs. The charm of possession and the allure of consumption of objects lose appeal and significance in the land of plenty. The individual can have what he needs to live comfortably without being preoccupied by it. At such times, the Doing personality focuses attention on another level of concern. The need to redefine oneself, to discover one's identity, and to experience the world in all its richness becomes important at the level of Doing. Self-expression, creativity, and a sense of social consciousness take on importance. Doing man genuinely *needs* to rediscover himself, to reintegrate his personality around new principles, and to concern himself with the pursuit of knowledge, self-expression, and compassion. Other people become increasingly important, not as means to ends, possessions, or articles of satisfaction, but as role models, personalities, and objects of mutual regard. The various advantages and pitfalls of the Doing personality will be examined in Chapter Five.

The highest level of need orientation is that of the Being level. As strange as it may seem, though the Being level individual is no longer oriented to physical and lower psychological needs—he has organized his life and fully integrated his personality—he too has a level of need orientation. Being man needs to show compassion and warmth to others; he literally finds enlightenment in giving wisdom, help, food, and shelter—whatever is necessary. The bodhisattva, the sage, and the saint are all renowned for their lives of selfless giving. This is the role of Being man. Thus, evolution best furthers itself by requiring the most advanced to take a part in bringing along the others.

In the continuum of Having, Doing, and Being, there are a number of signs of general progression, all characteristics of human psycho-spiritual development through all the stages. But there is an increasingly accelerated development from Having to Doing to Being. All of human moral and psychological evolution can be seen in terms of these indicators:

1) An expanded awareness of time, particularly with respect to the future. As the individual develops, the purview of temporal orientation widens so that the past and the future have greater significance and meaning in the present. This does not mean that the individual is unconcerned with the present. Quite to the contrary, the present is more comfortable, more amenable to the subject because it has meaning as part of a broader temporal context.

2) A progressive overcoming of the environment and a diminishing of the dependence of the self on external factors. This process is first apparent in the triumph of man over nature. Later, social and psychological factors become less critical. This is not to say that the enlightened man is less social, only that he is less dependent upon the social and psychological factors that preoccupy people at lower levels. At these higher levels, one becomes more resistant to unreflective enculturation.

3) An increasing appreciation of the world, the environment, or others, for themselves. Thus, independence from a thing is often correlative to a greater appreciation for and understanding of that thing. When nature threatens man, the relationship between man and nature is one of adversaries. But as he becomes free from nature's oft-violent exaction, man grows to understand nature for itself. The same holds true for man's relationship with others and with himself.

4) Following from the previous point, an increased sense of morality. A more objective sense of what is right, independent of what is expedient, evolves. When man begins looking outside of himself and appreciating the object for itself, what is right is no longer simply what is right *for him* but becomes something more expansive. Independence and understanding bring appreciation and respect for the integrity of the other, whether this other be animal, another human, or a foreign country.

Two points should be made in conclusion. First, it should be obvious from what has been said that the progressive continuum of development is not a downhill ride. Each phase of development has its own set of trials and tests. For example, the Doing level of development can at first be one of the most psychologically painful stages to undergo. A second consideration is the resurrection of lower needs, habits, or tendencies at higher levels. Often certain behaviors fill very different functions with higher level persons than may have been the case with lower levels. This phenomenon will be discussed at much greater length in the following chapters. It is now time to turn to a closer examination of the three levels of psycho-spiritual development: Having man, Doing man, and Being man.

4
Having Man

The more one possesses, the more one is possessed.
Nietzsche

As we have seen, on the tripartite scheme Having man is the most basic and essentially the "lowest" of the three types of personality orientation. He needs that which is tangible and can be possessed. He finds meaning in the possessory relationship and seeks to derive satisfaction, power, and prestige in the context of ownership.

There are basically two kinds of Havers. The first, the more primitive type, is less frequent in our society today than in the past. This kind of Haver is a result of poverty, lack of education, or any one of a number of other limiting social conditions. This is Mitchell's "Survivor" (Mitchell 1983, 5). In a sense, this type of individual is not a Haver at all but a "have not." The struggle to satisfy lower level needs such as for food, shelter, and adequate health care has left this individual without the time and energy to pursue higher needs. He is located at Maslow's deficit level of need fixation. His plight makes it quite clear that psychological development can only occur once satisfaction of lower-level physical needs can be maintained.

The second type of Having man is the relatively more populous strain, in fact, in many respects the hallmark of modern society, who will be readily recognized by the reader. He is contemporary consumeristic man, the product of the market economy and the advent of mass production. Though his lower level physical needs have been consistently satisfied from birth, the acquisition of things is still of paramount importance. This chapter will focus primarily on this type of personality.

As noted in Chapter Three, Having man derives self-identity from what he owns. In fact, if the existential situation of Havers could be summed up in a few words, it would be that the relationship between subject and world is best characterized as that of "possession." Often he seeks ownership precisely because he hopes to become associated or indued with the characteristics of the possessed object. An ancient analogue of this process can be seen in the very primitive ritual wherein early man believed that by actually consuming another animal, the characteristics of the animal would be transferred to the host. Thus, the eating of the heart of the lion was believed to transfer the beast's courage and strength to the one who ate it. Psychoanalysts have theorized that a modern equivalent of this takes place every Sunday all over the world in the doctrine of transubstantiation. The "body of Christ, blood of Heaven," as represented in the wafer and wine, is a contemporary symbolic attempt to take on the beneficent qualities of Christ.

In more profane contexts, a great deal of the modern economy is powered by the tendency of buyers to identify with a product. Thus, advertising seeks to indue a product with a set of perceived characteristics; the consumer will purchase it in an attempt to "become" that for which the product stands. Alvin Toffler has noted this tendency:

> An object, whether a car or a can opener, may be evaluated along many different parameters. A car, for example, is more than a conveyance. It is an expression of the personality of the user, a symbol of status, a source of that pleasure associated with speed. . . . The satisfaction a consumer gains from such factors may, depending on his values, outweigh the satisfaction he might receive from improved gas consumption or pickup power. . . .
>
> A traditional notion that each object has a single easily definable function clashes with all that we

> now know about human psychology, about the role of values in decision-making, and with ordinary common sense as well (Toffler 1970, 69).

The propensity to identify with objects or qualities of objects is much more pervasive than might be evident. By slipping on a shirt, using a new deodorant, buying a new car, the Haver, like the savage who consumes lion hearts, seeks to take on the properties he sees embodied in the products. But something *more* happens as well. It is not only that the product exudes a particular physical or psychological characteristic that is attractive to the Haver; the act of owning the object itself bestows a deep sense of control and satisfaction. It is as if Having man fears losing the quality—whether attractiveness, intelligence, healthiness, or whatever—or fears not being able successfully to manifest that quality in his own life. He seeks to retain the object associated with that quality, thus somehow ensuring his continued dominion over the quality.

Having man, however, is often the victim of a tragic irony. Like the lover who wants only what (whom) he can't have, so the very act of ownership by Havers drains the object of the sought-after quality. Just as Groucho Marx "wouldn't be a member of any club that would have me for a member," so Having man cannot extract peace, joy, or confidence from any object that he is capable of possessing. It is exactly this irony that makes the Haver's pursuit an unending one. The acquisitive instinct is not only insatiable; it is also the genesis of the long, enervating process that fuels the modern consumeristic economy, proliferating products at an exponential rate, and inculcating in the buyer the feeling that happiness can be found in a new toothpaste. Ultimately, when nothing is capable of lending satisfaction, the pursuit of ownership for itself becomes paramount. At this point, the person begins to acquire things of a kind, or in a quantity, that he will never use. The hoarding personality is characteristic of this syndrome.

One outstanding characteristic of the Having personality

is a low degree of psychological flexibility. This seems to be a natural result of finding one's self-identity and meaning in an array of ephemeral objects, which makes one's identity only as certain as the continued existence of the objects. The great social psychologist Hadley Cantril noted both the process of object-identification and the resultant psychological syndrome:

> Some people will regard certain objects with so great a value and will identify themselves so completely with these objects that it may be difficult to orient themselves in what might seem to the outside observer as the most intelligent or appropriate way. Just as a child may regard a toy or a particular corner of the room as part of him, just as some primitives regard their excrement or some possession as part of themselves, so do some men in our society identify themselves with their houses, their land or their fortunes.

Inflexibility is the result of this orientation.

> It therefore becomes impossible for such people to consider their own actions without thinking at the same time of the fate of the things that are also bound to them. Adjustment becomes less flexible, choices are more circumscribed. Thus, some penniless families living on marginal land which they call theirs will not move to richer soil provided them by the Resettlement Administration; some wealthy people may prefer to face the risk of revolution or dictatorship in which all their money would be confiscated, than pay larger taxes to ease the lot of the disgruntled workers (Cantril 1963, 37-38).

The second type of Having personality, the modern mass-consumer, reveals the inert nature of the Having personality. "Needs" proliferate proportionately to the availability of worthy objects of satisfaction. When a hundred different brands of breakfast cereal can be had, raw hunger gives way to taste. When styles of clothes change every season and available choice approaches legion, the utility of garments is replaced with fashion. In this manner, the consumeristic culture helps shape the personality that has satisfied basic needs in the Having style by multiplying the objects of identification and inculcating a feeling of "need." This situation will be discussed at greater length shortly.

Another interesting phenomenon also occurs at the Having level. Endeavors and activities originally developed in the culture as a response to higher needs may be subjugated to Having level ends. For example, religious activity is often used by the Haver to affect basically economic ends. Being seen in church may have advantageous results because others in a parish or congregation patronize the business of fellow church-goers. Modern psychologists have estimated that as many as ninety percent of all church-goers in the West are "extrinsically oriented" to religion, which is characteristic of the Having personality (Hunt and King 1977, 138-157).

Similarly, education may be seen by the Having personality as simply a means to the end of finding a job. Any theoretical or "esoteric" knowledge, anything that cannot command a large salary upon graduation, is deemed worthless. In this manner, Having man participates in a number of activities that might have originated to serve more developed need-functions but uses them toward possessory ends. (The converse of this situation will be examined in the next chapter, which will investigate how some individual pursuits and social institutions may have originally developed to fulfill lower needs but take on a different significance at more developed personality levels.)

Finally, in the Having personality the level of meaning is closely related to the level of need-fixation. Meaning for Having man is found in the act of possession and in the effort to own what one desires or admires. Meaning, in the existential sense of denoting the inquiry into a deeper significance, has not become an important concern for Having man.

In a Freudian context, if Having man suffers from any psychological problems in the usual sense, it is id-superego relationships which are most troublesome. Put in terms of common sense, the conflict between what is desired and what one in good conscience can have is a central issue to the Having personality. This must be contrasted with that of the Doing personality in whom ego conflicts, centering around the search for self-identity, are of greatest concern.

One measure of psychological growth, as outlined in the previous chapter, is a sense of continuity between past and present, along with an increased sense of power to guide the future. Having man is hopelessly present-oriented because the gratification of physical needs has a peculiarly evanescent quality. Physical pleasure experienced even a moment ago has no lasting effect into the present. Further, when meaning is gained by ownership, this ownership must be current. Finally, when self-identification occurs in the act of possessing the object, past or future possession implies the absence of such identification in the present. In short, the possession must be *now* or be void of psychological import. This situation is in radical contrast with that of Doing man, who may find vicarious meaning in a reminiscent moment —the memory of what he has experienced or at the thought of the successes he achieved earlier in life—thus fostering a more direct relationship with other times in one's life.

A second measure of individual development is the psychological, if not physical, emancipation from contingent external factors over which one has no control. Once again, Having man is the most vulnerable of psychological types because he finds his meaning and identity in things external to himself. While anyone could be physically incapacitated by the loss of a necessary tool or instrument, the personality that finds meaning in owning an object may be doubly burdened. Thus, the destruction of a sports car is more than the loss of a vehicle; it is the destruction of an important source of psychological self-identification and meaning.

An increasing appreciation of the other, whether another individual, another country, or the environment, is a third sign of psychological development. The Having personality ranks low on this dimension also. The Haver is often self-centered, authoritarian, xenophobic, and in short, relates to the world in terms of how it may further his own ends. He has no sense of duty except to himself or his own clan. He sees nature as something to be subjugated, and takes a similar attitude to those from other lands or cultures. In short, Having man cannot appreciate the other without *owning* it, and, since ownership by Havers entails an attempt at making the object part of the self, it is not the other that is appreciated at all.

The last general indicator of moral development is the emergence of an objective sense of right and wrong, independent of what might be most expedient to the subject. With Having man, put briefly, what is right is what is right *for him*. He fails to see the wider picture involved in any issue having more than one perspective. If there are two sides to an argument, it is certain that Having man sees only his side. This myopic tendency is most apparent in political and international affairs, where stakes are higher and historical and political factors are more easily obscured. It is not that the Haver is in bad faith or that he knows he is misconstruing a situation. Rather, it is simply that his judgment is genuinely skewed by his psychological orientation.

Morally, Having man has generally internalized a set of inflexible rules that tend to preserve the status quo and, if possible, the Haver's own interests. Further, it is important to note that though a Haver may be characterized as very self-centered morally, this self-centeredness may sometimes further admirable or altruistic goals. This is because a great deal of self-identification may occur with respect to an object which others consider as independent of the self. For example, a Haver with a high degree of identification with national concerns will be considered patriotic by others. Another Haver, who does not share this high level of self-identification with the nation at large, will view the first's willingness to risk his life as altruistic—not self-centered in the least—because this observer does not identify with the nation to the degree of the first. But the Haver who has a "possessory" interest in the nation is really engaged, in a psychological sense, in *self*-preservation. For him self-identification may include things such as family and nation that are perceived as "other" by many. Thus, a self-centered act might appear quite altruistic to another individual having a different focus of self-identification.

Insofar as loyalty to family and patriotism to one's nation are good and desirable things, Having man's behavior in these contexts is quite laudable. What is not so admirable is his need for a possessory relationship in order to be motivated. Because similar behavior is possible without the ownership of the object, qualities like patriotism, loyalty to family, and love for another take on a more majestic countenance at higher levels of psychological development.

In each of the four dimensions of psychological development, Having man displays a characteristic self-centered inflexibility to what he does not possess, either actually or psychologically. Politically he tends to be staunchly partisan and is often militaristic and imperialistic. In some respects, Havers make the best patriots. "My country, right or wrong" is an attitude characteristic of Having man. This trait is dangerous, however, when coupled with an authoritarian personality structure, as found in many Havers. The atrocities of the Nazis, carried out with the attitude that "I'm just following orders," is the deplorable progeny of this psychological orientation. Culturally, Having man is ethnocentric, xenophobic, and often exhibits a reactionary inertia with respect to changes in his own society. On the other hand, the Having orientation may sometimes provide a stable framework of "old-fashioned values" that may serve as a haven from the dizzying changes that are now occurring in the modern world.

Society at the Having Level

To what degree may a society's broad social, political, and economic tendencies reflect the psychological orientation of that culture's constituents? It is my position that, just as individual psychological development can be gauged by examining traits and behavior of the individual, the level of psycho-social development in a social unit can be assessed by analysis of the behaviors and institutions it embodies, or holds out as meaningful. Work, marriage, the form of religious devotion, education are but a few of the wide variety of indicators of this sort.

A great deal has been written about socialization, the internalizing of social norms, mores, and habits by the individual. Cantril's *The Psychology of Social Movements* is a classic introduction to the field. Consequently, it is not necessary to retrace the development of thought in this area over the past century. Rather, I simply wish to re-emphasize the reciprocal relationship between individual and society. Society influences personal development and, conversely, individuals often have profound effects on society. Societies—and individuals, for that matter—develop precisely because there is not a static relationship between the individual and his culture. Novelty enters in and helps bring about social evolution when individual patterns of thought and behavior change and influence the wider social milieu. What exactly causes a new pattern of behavior to gain acceptance in the society at large is the subject of a great deal of debate. But that society changes, no one can doubt in our era.

The concept that will elicit the most resistance, however, is that society *develops*. Development includes not only the concept of change, but the notion that society gets better. A great deal of twentieth-century cultural anthropology holds an opposite view, that no society can be judged as better than any other society because there is no set of absolute standards by which to judge. For example, while "success" might be of great importance in one culture, it is of no relevance in another. The problem with judging cultures different from our own, the argument goes, is that inevitably the judge finds himself utilizing those values that are most important in his own culture when he judges the other culture. We cannot know if objective evaluation is possible, the argument concludes, because we have no means of assessing the relative goodness of the differing values and institutions that are manifest in a culture.

This same argument has been directed to the individual as well. Cultural relativism becomes individual relativism when the judge decides that there is no way to weigh the values and behaviors of one person against those of another. Despite the relativist appeal, however, we *do* evaluate and pass judgment on others as part of the continuing maintenance of society. Laws do sanction standards to be applied to individual behavior, and without some standard, society would quickly disintegrate into Hobbes' state of nature.

Here I will simply assert as a necessary and fundamental axiom that there is a compelling standard by which to judge a society's relative development. The standard to be applied is the following: *A society's level of development—and thus its goodness—will be measured by the extent to which it fosters individual psycho-spiritual development for all those within it.* Individual psycho-spiritual development will in turn be measured by those schemes, theories, and hierarchies that view man as a progressive, evolving, ameliorative being. The Having-Doing-Being trichotomy is a simplified version of one such scheme. Explicit in this theory is the notion that this psycho-spiritual development cannot occur until the physical and economic needs of man have been met. In short, a society is functioning successfully to the degree that it allows the total person to develop.

Given this orientation, a society can be assessed by analyzing three factors: 1) the institutions it embodies; 2) the level at which these institutions operate; and 3) the extent to which these institutions, and the culture generally, are able to provide for the physical, economic, social, and psycho-spiritual well-being of its inhabitants, e.g., the effectiveness of these institutions. The independence of these dimensions demonstrates that it is possible for a society to be high-minded in its goals and yet ineffective in realizing the goals it mandates. For example, a society that emphasizes psycho-spiritual development without ensuring satisfaction of the lower physical needs would be wasting a great deal of resources, since an impoverished population would not be ready to move into the higher level of development manifest in its many cultural institutions. Many cultures in the East, particularly India, are reminiscent of this problem.

As cultures in the East have been high-minded but often ineffective, so the West has witnessed the opposite extreme. Here a wealth of resources has combined with an uninspiring view of humankind to create a psychologically stagnant social order. Our culture is very effective in achieving its designated ends, but those ends are subnormal, relative to the possible reaches of personal development. Thus both East and West, for their own respective reasons, have failed to evolve a social order that adequately furthers the development of the majority of their constituents.

Where does a Having society stand in the continuum of social development? As with individuals, there are basically two types of Having social orders. The first is the poor culture that has failed, either because of natural or social constraints, to ensure the most basic needs of those within it. Nothing but economic development can ameliorate conditions in this type of society. Insofar as a major portion of the Third World currently subsists in such a state, a majority of the world's population has not evolved beyond the lowest of developmental stages. Lifting these peoples from this primitive level constitutes the most significant moral and political problem to be confronted in the next century.

The second type of Having society is the wealthy society that fosters the production and consumption of goods as an end in itself. It is a society that fulfills the lower needs of its workers and citizens and then creates new though similar needs, where the apotheosis of consumerism corresponds with a neglect of higher needs. Futurist Alvin Toffler, author of *Future Shock*, has written of the diversification of needs in the affluent society:

> In a society of scarcity, needs are relatively universal and unchanging because they are starkly related to the "gut" function. As affluence rises, however, human needs become less directly linked to biological survival and more highly individualized. Moreover, in a society caught up in complex, high-speed change, the needs of the individual—which arise out of his interaction with the external environment—also change at relatively high speed. The more rapidly changing the society, the more temporary the needs. Given the general affluence of the new society, he can indulge many of these short-term needs (Toffler 1970, 70).

Despite this "individualized" need tendency, the diversification spreads horizontally to other Having needs, rather than vertically to higher level needs. The Having society is marked not only by its propensity to further the proliferation of tangible goods in all areas; it also rewards the Haver. Thus, the wealthy often ascend to positions of prestige and power in the community, being the model of success in the Having society.

The picture is considerably complicated by the fact that certain institutions may have originally arisen for higher motives and in response to higher-level needs, but are put to use in lower-level capacities. The extrinsic orientation to religion has been cited as an example of this. Conversely, some institutions may have arisen as a response to lower-level needs, only to be utilized for a wholly different set of needs. For example, marriage in many cultures, particularly here in the West, seems to have given the male a possessory interest in his wife. Even less than a century ago, a woman still was, in many significant legal respects, "owned" by her husband. Yet today marriage has taken on a different countenance in modern society. There are still obvious sexual motives for marriage—though this is less significant today due to the prevalence of premarital sex—but there are other motives as well, including the attempt to prove one's maturity or to find one's identity. Though even these may be poor reasons for marriage, they are nonetheless expressions of higher psychological yearnings.

In the end, any society must be judged by observing the types of rewards it holds out for its constituents as representative of the good life. These expressions can be found in the structure of its laws, in its advertising, in the pronouncements of its leaders, heroes, and entertainers, and perhaps most importantly, in the everyday habits and customs of everyday people.

The affluent Having culture in many respects embodies the halcyon limbo between the poverty of the primitive Having culture and the psychological turbulence of the early Doing level of existence. This stage of culture may be seen as a time of self-centered rejuvenation, of gathering energy for what will be a soul-searching period of radical psychological re-evaluation and reconstruction at the Doing level. Having culture is, in almost every way, the existential calm before the storm.

5
Doing Man

We are neurotic to the extent that we are self-less.
Abraham Maslow

A survey of the most influential literature of the past century-and-a-half reveals two pervasive and commonly recurring themes or motifs that portray the psychology of twentieth-century life in the most revealing light. These are the sense of a loss of personal identity, along with the corresponding hope for the rediscovery of the self, and the desacralization of existence, accompanied by the corresponding search for meaning in life. The tone of this body of literature is not hopeful. From existentialists to the apologists of science, these works embody an overwhelming sense of futility and utter despair. This intellectual environment witnessed Camus as he asked his most fundamental question: "There is but one truly serious philosophical problem and that is suicide. Judging whether life is or is not worth living amounts to answering the fundamental question of philosophy." Apparently, more people than ever today answer this most fundamental question in the negative, following with the "appropriate" action. While on the international front we are confronted with famine, perpetual war, and the seemingly imminent possibility of nuclear disaster, the prognosis on the inner psychological front ranges from nihilism to determinism to reckless hedonism. Even a usually optimistic humanist like Clarence Darrow, who fought many a courtroom battle to further the dictates of individual liberty and intellectual progress, remarked, "Life is an unpleasant interruption of nothing. The best thing you can say about it is that it doesn't last too long."

Depth pessimism is "in" as the human condition is characterized in a plethora of ways from anguish to alienation and from disillusionment to self-deception. Life has been depicted as a room with no exit, or even as a wall. By most social prophets, man has been inexorably condemned to live naked amid the opulence, a creature of bright lights and nervous jest orbiting a searching, empty void. And perhaps, at first glance, this is understandable. The faded eighteenth-century hope that a new age of enlightenment—spirited in on the wings of technological progress and the promised blessings of plenty for all the world—has left in its stead only disillusion. This is a time when many acknowledge the seductive glamor of the nihilistic decree that life *means* something, because we *know* it means nothing. Many believe the best thing an education can secure is the knowledge that we are totally ignorant of the reason for our existence. It is at the very nexus of these issues that we find Doing man.

In the most general way, Doing man is identified by two outstanding characteristics. First, there is an emphasis on living a life rich with a variety of experiences. He strives to experience himself and the world in as many different states, modes, and situations as possible. In the early stages, he even seeks to be as many different people as possible. The Doer embraces no moral code except for Camus' "ethic of quantity," by which life is lived at the level of doing the greatest number of different things. By this canon, the *quality* of life is simply a function of the *quantity* of experience.

The second prevailing characteristic of Doing man is his search for psychological integration and for a deepened sense of meaning in life. He seeks a renewed feeling of the sacred, a revitalized outlook on life, and a strong and flexible self-identity from which to operate, psychologically speaking. The Doer seeks to transcend previous modes of self-perception, establish a novel sense of self, and to escape twentieth-century *angst* by making peace with self, God, and world.

These two characteristics of Doing man have at once a complementarity and a tension. The impulse toward a great variety of experiences is necessary to avail the personality of possible new modes of self-orientation. And such a person, in identifying with these diverse experiences, is conducting a brand of psychological window-shopping, "trying on" new experiences and lifestyles in an attempt to see which comports with his more fundamental personal attributes and goals. In short, this individual seeks a pattern, a mold, into which to pour his life. Thus, the individual not inclined to academic pursuits would be unlikely to adopt the lifestyle pattern of the intellectual. Similarly, the person with an athletic inclination would be influenced by life patterns most consistent with recreational and sports-related activity. The "trying on" of these diverse experiences allows the individual to discard those patterns of activity and self-identification that are inconsistent with his basic traits and dispositions and, conversely, to select and incorporate those elements that are to become the locus for self-identification. This allows integration of those lifestyle elements that are in accord with the basic characteristics of the individual, thus satisfying the drive toward self-identity and meaning.

At the same time, however, experience-seeking may lead to fragmentation of the personality rather than integration. Protean man emerges as the psychic progeny of this situation. In the words of contemporary psychologist Robert Jay Lifton:

> I should like to examine a set of psychological patterns characteristic of contemporary life, which are creating a new kind of man—a "protean man." As my stress is upon change and flux, I shall not speak much of "character" and "personality," both of which suggest fixity and permanence. . . . For it is quite possible that even the image of personal identity, in so far as it

> suggests inner stability and sameness, is derived from a vision of a traditional culture in which man's relationship to his institutions and symbols is still relatively intact—which is hardly the case today. If we understand the self to be the person's symbol of his own organism, then self-process refers to the continuous psychic re-creation of that symbol (Lifton 1970, 28).

Doing man, particularly in the early stages, is the modern-day Proteus. His psychological flexibility often reaches the extreme of lifestyle schizophrenia, as the Doer is particularly vulnerable to environmental stimuli, which offers a new way of living or of seeing himself. The process is characterized by "an interminable series of experiences and explorations—some shallow, some profound—each of which may be readily abandoned in favor of still new psychological quests." The subject is ripe and ready for change; the problem, however, is what to change *to*. The pain of this so-called identity crisis makes the plight of this individual particularly poignant in a culture where experience is mass produced and mass consumed. The subject craves experiences as a means to self-worth, a feeling of psychological maturity, and a sense of identity. The more quickly experiences are offered by a society capable of the mass production of events that yield such experience, and the more readily they are consumed by the personality seeking self-legitimation, the more surely the Doer will "lose himself" in the whirl of the constantly changing activity around him.

Modern Doing man may thus become psychologically marooned at a stage where an escalating cycle of experience leaves no time for the integration of this experience. This is modern Proteus, a personality bereft of a center locus of experience, who temporarily molds himself, his behavior, and his mode of self-expression to the context in which he finds himself. He is the adaptor, capable of changing chameleon-like in response to a new situation or environmental stimulus. He is at best an affable, flexible, easy-going socialite who prides himself on getting along in any given situation. At worst he is the master of disguise and a man without identity who, when his situationally imposed mask is removed, possesses no substance underneath.

Doing man at this early stage is by nature slavishly aware of what other people are thinking and doing. But he is not simply sensitive to information for its own sake. Instead, he continually seeks acceptance by emulating others and by identifying with what he perceives as influential to the herd. And while it is true that context-oriented Proteus is a "conformist" of sorts, his behavior often does not comport with the traditional concept of conformity. Indeed, he is often the radical nonconformist with respect to those norms embodied in the middle-class, nine-to-five social ethic. But he conforms to some other perceived pattern of individual behavior just the same. Often this behavior will be in strict accord with the prescribed, though unwritten, norms of a subcult. An example is the hippie who advocates complete freedom of dress, practicing his belief by sporting long hair, beads, and ripped jeans, who negates his own credo, criticizing those who choose to dress in more traditional ways, denouncing the suit and tie as "square." While Doing man is not often this hypocritical in his approach to life, he nonetheless plays the part of the conforming nonconformist and the shadow behind the mask. Differing situations bring about a shift in his personal orientation. In short, the environment is the independent variable and the individual the dependent one.

The conspicuous consumption of experience, promoted by the media and underwritten by our modern economy, has also contributed to what has been called the "existential malaise" of the present century. Jung writes that of all the successful middle-aged patients he treated, there was not one who suffered, at the most fundamental level, from anything other than the sense of a lack of meaning in life. Everyday existence appears banal because of a general lack of commitment to social and individual growth, widespread apathy in the political and international spheres, and even a loss of self-confidence in the sciences and humanities. In philosophy, the most general and important arena of human understanding, "philosophers no longer explain the nature of things or pretend to tell us how to live," in the words of social critic Christopher Lasch.

In this emotional and intellectual milieu, modern Doing man confronts his own existence, seeking answers to the biggest question: What is the meaning of my life? Nietzsche said, "He who has a *why* to live can bear with almost any *how*." It seems that in an age of psychological alienation and epistemic relativism, however, answers to the questions of why are in short supply.

Amid the banality of everyday existence, one finds poignance in the myth of Sisyphus, the timeless saga of a giant condemned to endlessly repeating a task that can never be completed. Sisyphus must spend eternity rolling his boulder to the top of a hill, from where it will roll back again. This is taken to be a metaphor for contemporary existence. But modern Doing man is not poised at his rock, preparing himself for another soul-weakening push up to the precipice from where the stone will tumble back down of its own weight. Whatever else it is, the life of Doing man is not repetitive; indeed, just the opposite is true. The Doer lives a life of random diversity. He is not stationed at his mountain, condemned to a certain, though incompletable, task. No, it is much worse. At the early stage of rampant experience-seeking, Doing man is sentenced to search the world over, no place being sacred or even profane, but rather all places being ensconced in a limbo between the two. And there is no set task, no object or pursuit toward which to strive. Where Sisyphus' goal is impossible to complete, modern Doing man at the early level has no goal at all. His is a life full of content and devoid of form. There is endless choice and no reason to choose. The old gods thought they had fabricated the most severe of punishments in answer to the insolence of Sisyphus, but they were wrong. The modern gods—the experience-makers, the media and consumeristic culture itself—surely have fashioned a far more inhuman fate for Doing man.

It is in this self-less void that modern Proteus and Sisyphus are merged in the quest for experience and the imperative to find meaning. But, as we have seen, these two drives may be antithetical to one another. Deep existential meaning—the only kind of meaning that will suffice at this stage—is impossible without integration. Integration is impossible in a long string of temporary pseudo-identifications and changes from one lifestyle to another, in which Doing man swings from experience to experience in a futile attempt to find the only true experience—selfhood.

Consumption and Integration of Experience

As we have seen, Doing man has a propensity to identify with new experiences, images, and lifestyles, but cannot integrate these into his personality. Toffler convincingly argues that the situation will only become worse in the future:

> To be "between styles" or "between subcults" is a life-crisis, and the people of the future spend more time in this condition, searching for styles, than do the people of the past or present. . . . Restless movement from subcult to ephemeral subcult describes the arc of [such a person's] life. . . .
>
> There are plenty of reasons for the restlessness. It is not merely that the individual's psychological needs change more often than in the past; the subcults also change. For this and other reasons, as subcults become more unstable, the search for a personal style will become increasingly more intense, even frenetic in the decades to come (Toffler 1970, 316).

Further, as noted, there exists a reciprocal relationship between individual and society such that cultural movements reinforce individual trends, which in turn fuel widespread production of fads, fashions, and lifestyles at the social level. Supply escalates with demand as cultural diversity feeds individual insecurity, which in turn fosters an increase in the demand for lifestyle options. Some of these lifestyles—literally patterns of psycho-social behavioral organization—will become popular for a while, providing a widespread flash-in-the-pan locus for individual self-identification. The whole process comes to resemble a perverse cultural version of chance variation and natural selection.

But why should cultural diversity prevent psychological integration? Why should not the converse be true? For example, why should not expanding the available lifestyle options increase the possibilities for individual psychological development, giving more people a greater choice of potential role models and living patterns? The answer, basically, is that it does so for those who are adept enough, or perhaps lucky enough, to make the switch from experience-consumption to experience-integration. But it is more difficult today to make this psychological switch, and when it does happen, it often takes considerable time. The media-rich environment of our culture contributes to the prevalence of the so-called "identity crisis." Increased economic and intellectual freedom does so as well (see Chapter Eight). As education augments the imagination of the individual, and as monetary independence and other social factors delay the time when the subject is forced to commit to a life goal, a greater variety of experiences may be had.

While there are undoubtedly greater rewards for those who are able to integrate their personalities at the Doing level in our age, the chance that any given individual will do so is considerably reduced. There are two basic reasons for this. First, the selected pattern of integration must be consistent with the more fundamental capacities and propensities of the individual. In other words, lifestyle patterns must fit individual desires, talents, and goals. A physically handicapped individual will probably not successfully integrate his personality around the concept of athleticism. Second, the selected pattern must be both consistent with itself and all-embracing enough to include all of the drives, talents, and desires of the personality. If the lifestyle of the artist is adopted, for example—if the individual lives his life in a manner that he believes to comport in all of its facets with what he thinks artists do—certain aspects of this pattern may clash with other drives or talents. Long hours of practicing the piano leave little time for football with the boys, and the fingers must not be threatened by an injury resulting from sports play. If the individual wishes both art and sports, the pattern of the artist is incomplete and inadequate. Integration, adoption of a single lifestyle pattern, can then occur only at the price of abandoning a part of one's personality.

The other option available is the adoption of a pattern that is inconsistent with itself. A person cannot be both a bon vivant and a mystic if the subject believes the mystic must reject worldly pleasures. Any lifestyle pattern that attempts to combine these two contradictory schemes will probably fail. And though other combinations seem less contradictory in a logical sense, nonetheless there are vast problems with living life fully in two lifestyles simultaneously.

Psychological integration thus demands both comprehensiveness and consistency. Insofar as no pattern of integration is likely to meet both these demands entirely, we have the psychological correlate of Godel's theorem (which holds that mathematical systems can be complete only at the cost of inconsistency, or consistent at the cost of comprehensiveness). Completeness without repression in the personality can come only at the expense of contradiction.

Having outlined these general psychological principles, an answer is possible for the query: Why does the consumption of experience preclude psychological integration? It is because experience-consumption—the random movement from experience to experience, temporarily identifying with each particular experience as it comes along—does not require the individual to construct a comprehensive pattern of self-identity. One part of the personality may be satisfied at one time with one particular experience, and another part at another time with some other experience. The experience is itself mistaken for the self; i.e., it is believed to provide a pattern for the entire personality. If the subject can be an artist now and an athlete later, a lover of fine wines now and an ascetic later, an intellectual now and an ignoramus later, there is no need to construct a comprehensive self-identity. Further, the greater the number of experiences that can be consumed, the more specific satisfaction becomes to a particular fragment of personality. The more often each fragment takes on an autonomous quality due to repeated gratification, the less likely self-integration becomes.

This explains why early Doing man, characterized by contradictory tendencies, exhibits the psychological properties he does. His inner world is marked by an ambivalence that at once celebrates his uniqueness and desperately seeks to fit in; he clings to his independence and looks for commitment; he is both wildly extravagant in his modes of self-expression, style, and dress, and at the same time extremely self-conscious. The greatest disadvantage in this orientation, aside from the fact that the personality is not allowed to progress to stages with greater rewards, is that there is always conflict and uncertainty in new situations requiring a patterned response. The subject is literally torn between which "me" to utilize in the predicament at hand. Should the athlete or the intellectual handle this? Also, situations may arise that place two or more elements of the personality in direct conflict with one another, yet there is no supervening sense of identity to legislate a response.

The distinction between lifestyle consumption and lifestyle integration is actually a difference in degree, rather than a difference in kind. The two polar extremes of consumption and integration lie along a continuum on which a given personality can be plotted. Integration will usually be accompanied with a certain amount of incompleteness; consumption will come with inconsistency. But what really sets the integrated personality, at the later

Doing level, apart from the consumptive personality, at the earlier stages, and how can they be distinguished? The problem is more difficult than it might at first appear. No personality is unidimensional; thus, no one will act in a similar way in all situations. Even the integrated personality adapts to differing circumstances, responding differently in diverse contexts. Conversely, no personality is completely fragmented. Though there are many different "me" identities which appear in different experiences, seldom if ever does this proliferation of identities reach the extreme where there is a different identity for each and every experience.

There are two prevailing characteristics of the integrated personality: a low level of psychological compartmentalization and a high level of selectivity of lifestyle fragments. Conversely, the experience-consumer has a high level of compartmentalization and a low level of fragment selectivity. For example, suppose there is an individual whom we will call Victor who is attracted to two seemingly contradictory lifestyle orientations. Victor is, on one hand, interested in highly intellectual pursuits and self-development. He loves the arts, books, and is interested in yoga and meditation. At the same time, however, suppose Victor loves nightlife, varied lovers, and the avid pursuit of the "gentlemen's art of inebriation." If Victor perceives no conflict between these two general types of activities, then there will be no problem of integration. In reality there may be grave problems with the combination, but this will not trouble Victor from the standpoint of reconciling these seemingly disparate drives if he does not recognize the conflict.

It is more likely, however, that Victor, being intelligent and perceptive, will experience a conflict between his two types of interest. He now has a choice. He may simply repress one of the interests. For example, he may choose to abandon the life of the socialite in favor of that of the spiritual adept. This would be an unsatisfactory response, however. Modern psychology from Freud onward is replete with the unhappy results of repression. Victor may, on the other hand, remain a lifestyle consumer. He may spend half of his time doing what the socialite does and the other half with higher pursuits. This is the Protean or "context oriented" response discussed earlier. In this case, Victor will probably evince two completely separate types of behaviors in the two situations. He will drink, carouse, and socialize by night and follow his higher inclinations by day. This option is also an unfortunate response. First, as a practical matter, it is unlikely that Victor will do very well in either situation. Drinking into the early hours of the morning on a regular basis is not conducive to the mental concentration necessary to the scholar or meditator. Second, situations will arise in which the two lifestyles may be brought into conflict, in which Victor is subject to the uncertainty in deciding which "me" to put forward. Finally, such a patent conflict is psychologically destructive and precludes the stable sense of self and deeper sense of meaning that can appear only upon integration.

Victor's third alternative is the only satisfactory response. He must integrate the diverse elements of his personality into a comprehensive whole such that the satisfaction of one drive will *enhance* rather than detract from the expression of his other drives.

In order to effect integration, Doing man must first break down the barriers which compartmentalization fosters. Compartmentalization is simply the tendency to satisfy certain drives or aspects of the personality at certain times in a certain manner, and then to satisfy other drives at other times, keeping these isolated from each other. It is important to understand the function of each set of behaviors. If, for example, an interest in night life serves the function of allowing expression of the social drive in Victor's case, then he should develop other avenues for socializing. Incorporating social expression into his previously disparate intellectual or self-developmental behavior will greatly advance decompartmentalization. This decompartmentalizing is absolutely necessary for integration.

The second step in the process of integration is selecting certain favorable aspects of a pattern while leaving out other aspects. The most distinguishing characteristic of persons who are not integrated is the incorporation of an entire perceived role pattern into the personality. In other words, the experience consumer will adopt *all* of the perceived characteristics of the role he is attempting to emulate. For example, if the subject wishes to "be" the intellectual, he will change his entire pattern of style, behavior, and appearance in accordance with what he believes to be that of the intellectual, which may include a radical transition in dress, manner of speech, and a shift in other kinds of behavior. The integrated personality, on the other hand, extracts only those elements that are essential in fulfilling his particular psychological or behavioral goal. He is discriminating and does not accept or incorporate broad stereotypes, psychologically speaking. In the case of Victor, the process of selective integration means he might continue his nightlife, but as a teetotaler. An integrated person is thus a more complicated individual, fusing different elements of personality from diverse sources and incorporating them into a synthetic whole which will be expressed in every action.

These two elements—decompartmentalization and the selective process of incorporating only certain elements of a perceived pattern of style—mark the integrated personality. The subject has been "homogenized" so that there is a consistency and integrity of personality and expression in diverse situations.

However, personal integration can only occur when potential lifestyle patterns are brought into conformity with the subject's basic talents, desires, and capacities, and with each other.

Self-Actualization

The reader will recall that the three dimensions of psycho-spiritual development can be measured by:

1) what the subject identifies with; 2) which needs he concentrates on; and 3) what is meaningful to him. Early Doing man identifies himself in what he has done and whom he has known. The fleeting nature of this type of self-identification leads only to psychological instability and contradiction. Though diverse thinkers such as Sartre and Lifton seem to indicate that this is man's natural state in a culture such as ours, in which the subject is literally swamped with information to choose from and internalize, this "experiential transcendence" is only one phase in the great spectrum of self-identification. The integrated personality, on the other hand, is marked by a less frenetic mode of psychic existence, in which the subject is strongly committed and motivated by the great psychological power he has won from the struggle for identity. This modern-day psychic rite of passage separates those destined for higher psycho-spiritual rewards from those who will remain constant only in that they are constantly changing.

The level of need-fixation also varies through the Doing level. During the early stages, Doing man is torn between the need for self-legitimation through varying experiences and the need to found a permanent self. The Doer literally *needs* to transcend the flux of psychic existence, as the inchoate self strives for greater psychic perfection. Toward the latter stages of the Doing level, the subject's interests often turn outward to an external cause. Devotion to this object—whether a social movement, the welfare of other people, an abstract idea, or the love of God—sometimes leads to self-actualization, to be discussed shortly.

Finally, the imperative to self-legitimation intimately involves the quest for meaning in life. This search for authenticity, for what is real or true in life, often leads the subject through a series of patterns of experience which may include adherence to varying ideologies and lifestyle patterns, as well as widespread experimentation with sex and drugs. (In Chapter Eight some modern trends will be examined as they relate to this urge.) Finally, with integration comes a satisfaction with oneself, accompanied by the realization that true meaning can be found only through commitment rather than through transience, and that the ethic of quantity is ultimately a hindrance to actualizing the good life. It is only when this sense of meaning in life is realized that Camus' most "fundamental question" is answered wholeheartedly in the affirmative—life *is* worth living.

At the furthest reaches of the Doing level, and ultimately the culmination of this stage, awaits what Maslow has called "self-actualization." Actualization was discussed at some length in Chapter Two; the chief distinguishing characteristics of the self-actualized individual will be briefly reviewed here. First, self-actualization may occur only after all of the lower-level needs have been fulfilled. Higher psychological development thus stands on the edifice of physical, economic, social, and emotional satisfaction. Self-actualization is the realization of man's true potential; it is the clearing away of psychic impediments, and implies that psychopathology is the result of an unnatural frustration of our innermost nature.

Characteristics of actualized people include the following: They are realistically oriented. They accept themselves, others, and the world as they are, though this should not be confused with a complacent unwillingness to change things. They are spontaneous and problem-centered rather than self-centered. They commonly exhibit an air of emotional detachment and a need for privacy. They are autonomous and independent, identify strongly with mankind, and have a democratic character structure by which all individuals are perceived as equal, despite differences in status, achievement, or utility to society. Most have had profound mystical experiences, though these are not necessarily religious in character. Self-actualized people tend to resist conformity with society and environment and, as a result, appreciate others in original rather than stereotyped ways. Their relationships with a lucky few are emotional and profound. They are creative, do not confuse means with ends, and exhibit a sense of humor which is detached, even philosophical, but not hostile (Hall 1957).

These characteristics convey a development in the four criteria of psychological evolution discussed in the previous two chapters. Doing man, at his zenith, is psychologically independent of the environment to the extent that his self-identity is not a mere function of the social context in which he finds himself. He is still dependent to the extent that he takes his identity from a pattern he has constructed, which includes his role in society, devotion to a cause, or some other intangible external object. This relative self-stability indues him with a strength and independence that increasingly allow him to appreciate the other. At the higher reaches, this includes a detached, objective, and autonomous sense of right and wrong. Morality ceases to be a matter of functional social utility and becomes instead a genuine appeal to Kant's categorical imperative and Christ's Golden Rule. Finally, Doing man lives a life that is less a series of isolated present-moments and more a continuous moving picture. Orientation toward experience is a time-binding activity. Memories of experiences, successes, and life events are somehow more tangible, or perhaps simply more consoling, than memories of things owned. And with a high degree of integration comes a pattern of identity into which all of life's separate moments find meaning and a place within the larger mosaic of existence. Self-actualizers are to be found among the ranks of higher level Doers.

As noted in Chapters One and Two, the concept of self-actualization has many historical antecedents in the writings of sundry philosophers and psychologists. The concept elaborated here, along with the characteristics just listed, come from the work of Maslow. But implicit in this scheme are ideas from others as well. From Jung comes the idea of integrating disparate parts of the personality. Where Jung emphasized conscious and unconscious, persona and shadow, anima and animus, however, I have restricted my analysis to elements encountered consciously, often proliferated by the media, which offer patterns of style and behavior that the subject may "plug into." Integration may occur at a subliminal level as well, as Jung and others suggest. Another notion implicit in this discussion of self-actualization is that true understanding brings only goodness from human beings, as was taught by Plato, Aristotle, Spinoza, and others. This understanding requires not merely education in its contemporary sense, but a deep insight into oneself and a commitment to psycho-spiritual, not merely intellectual, development. Maslow's belief that human nature is basically good, that the socialized forms of psychopathology—hatred, racism, warfare, and alienation—are the result of obstacles on the road to selfhood, is characteristic. In clearing away these psychological obstacles, the individual opens the frontiers to complete development. Meaning and happiness are accompanied by virtue as the individual realizes his psycho-spiritual manifest destiny.

In a very real sense, Doing man at his highest reaches is the altruistic, self-divested, fully integrated and motivated individual admired by all of history, philosophy, and in its greater moments, psychology. He combines all of the virtues of outward confidence, creativity, and success with the subjective vision and equanimity befitting a platonic ruler. Despite this, however, even self-actualized individuals—who by Maslow's estimate constitutes less than one percent of the population in the West—do not embody the "farther reaches of human nature." Another level awaits—Being man.

Doing Level and Society

As noted in the previous two chapters, the tripartite scheme may be used not only to gauge the development of individuals, but may in a very real sense allow us to map the progress of a given society. A society is measured in its development: 1) by the types of habits, mores and institutions it embodies; 2) by the level at which these operate; and 3) by the extent to which the socially prescribed "good life" is fostered by these cultural patterns and institutions. Because many of these patterns are best exemplified by those of twentieth-century Western society, and because understanding these is so important to understanding the current psychosocial malaise, Chapters Seven and Eight are devoted to their investigation. It will be suggested at that time that modern American culture combines elements of the Having and Doing orientations.

One further general point should be made. Often individuals maintain old patterns of behavior even after psycho-spiritual ascent has been made. Old behavior comes to have a different function at the higher level. Similarly, institutions within a culture may have originally evolved to meet one set of needs and then later, after transition from lower to higher levels of development, come to express or satisfy other needs. For example, the sexual drive is a fundamentally physical deficit need. While sexual release is not, strictly speaking, essential to survival for the individual, it is a "physical" need in the sense that a number of biological and physiological processes are dependent on it, e.g., hormone levels rise with prolonged abstinence, endomorphines are released during sex, etc. Though sex is fundamentally a physical phenomenon, it is also used as a psychological expression on the Doing level. Thus, sexual activity comes to represent maturity, virility, or confidence. Sartre believed that sexual intercourse is the one true act in which the ego most completely dominates the will of another; the mystique of sex for him is the result of the psychological significance of the control of one and the vulnerability of the other. Of course, sex is also often used as an expression of love or devotedness. Finally, it is sometimes simply an "event legitimizer"—an experience had for itself, which the subject consumes as part of his pursuit of the ethic of quantity. All of these different motives are expressions at the level of Doing, of experience consumption or integration.

This process whereby one behavior may express and satisfy needs on a number of different levels occurs in many other areas. Eating, gathering together in social groups, and finding or constructing shelter are examples. What is important in analyzing this is not simply to look at the behavior but, more significantly, to examine how that behavior is being used, both individually and socially.

As we move to the third and highest level of human psycho-spiritual development, the road of modern science abruptly vanishes into the wilderness, leaving only a barely trodden footpath. The few markings along the way, left by the true adventurers of the spirit, are all that chart the course at this level. Traditional psychological concepts give way to more recondite and seemingly contradictory descriptions of experience. What are obscure, tautological abstractions to the many are profound, empirically experienced insights to the few. Deep in this black forest we find Being man.

6
Being Man

> Blessedness is not the reward of right
> living; it is the right living itself.
>
> Spinoza

> It is wisdom to know others.
> It is enlightenment to know one's self.
>
> Lao Tzu

To those who have never had a peak experience, much less permanently entered some realm of psychological transcendence, the contents of this chapter may seem quite perplexing. I must confess that, at one time, I eschewed any talk of transcending the subject/object dichotomy and many other "incredible" notions as fantastic flights of whimsy, to be grouped into the same class as seances, Ouiji boards, and the search for the soul of so-and-so last seen at a neighborhood tavern. I felt that any discourse on the matter should be properly prefixed with the "Yes, Virginia . . . " of another, similar topic, for these are "scientific" times.

I have changed my mind on some of these issues, for a number of reasons, however. First, it seemed to me that one should be able to develop one's personality in the same manner the physical body is developed. Meditation and other forms of psycho-spiritual training might be considered the marathon of the mind, pushing oneself to limits heretofore impossible, being what one could never be before. This general intuition was fostered by my wide reading in the areas of psychology, meditation, and mysticism. It seemed to me there are simply too many accounts of similar experiences from diverse eras and locales to ignore them. The literature of the East is, of course, famous for its emphasis on the "farther reaches" of human personality. But there are plenty of writers in the West who recount similar experiences. From Plotinus, Meister Eckhart, St. John, and St. Teresa, to name but a few, the lineage runs into our own century and includes the writings of Franklin Merrell-Wolff. Though there are what seemed to be individual differences in the various accounts, there is a great similarity in the general description of the psychological state elaborated. Even this, however, may not have convinced me. But when systematic studies indicated that a large number of everyday people, now living, have had similar peak experiences, the possibility began to look plausible. Finally, when a number of scientific studies revealed that Zen monks, practitioners of meditation techniques, and adepts in various disciplines demonstrate characteristic psychophysiological responses that are different from ordinary individuals, the evidence was convincing.

In the course of some of this investigation, I asked a colleague what he thought of the claims of meditators and mystics from all over the world. I remarked that if all of these claims were false, these people must all be either "crazy, confused, or lying." His response, quite characteristic of those in academic philosophy and psychology today, was to retort, "All of the above. They're crazy, confused, and they're lying on top of it!"

In the course of this chapter, I will be writing (and I presume most will be reading) from a vantage point somewhere "outside" that which is the subject of our interest. Still, a good many of us may have had profound though momentary experiences resembling some of the ones described in the literature. A greater number will have witnessed more subtle, gradual, everyday changes which give one a right to look forward to even more profound psycho-spiritual changes in the future. In short, many will have empirically verified to their own satisfaction the possibility for such experience, a possibility easily rejected by those who have not experimented with any psycho-spiritual technique. Being man, the third and highest model can be better understood by those who have had transcendent moments.

The advent of Being man heralds a radical transition in personal orientation and psychological motivation. The paradigms of Western psychology will and *must* be modified and extended to include this, the most noble form of human potentiality. To those who remain skeptical, two points should be addressed. First, skepticism is a healthy and vital attitude. But if a claim can be verified or rejected empirically, skepticism should not prevent the experiment from taking place. Let me simply invite the skeptics—dare them, if you will—to experience for themselves what here can be conveyed only vicariously. These preliminary experiences may reveal, in inchoate and transitory form, what appears to be a more or less permanent state for Being man. Further, in a world where true spiritual achievement is infrequent, we can find solace and inspiration in the words of Spinoza: "How would it be possible, if salvation is ready to our hands, and could without great labor be found, that it should be by almost all men neglected? But all things excellent are as difficult as they are rare."

Three Theories of Enlightenment

Attempts to put the arcane and seldom-experienced process of ultimate self-realization into Western paradigmatic terms have been increasingly popular in the last twenty years. Unfortunately, the theories are often as obscure or "metaphysical" as anything written by the sages of old. There is the problem of disparity between the Eastern and Western world views, and the misunderstanding is only amplified by the fact that transcendent experiences are often unintelligible to the "unemancipated." Notions of "ego death" and "subject/object transcendence" are incomprehensible, if not frightening, as the range of phenomenal experience and conceptual understanding of the uninitiated does not encompass such ideas. Indeed, it might be tempting to heed the admonition of the Buddha to forget metaphysics and simply get to work on self-transformation. But insofar as we seek a Western understanding of phenomena that have been traditionally cast in Oriental terms, I will address the most difficult of all states to conceptualize—enlightenment.

As noted in Chapter Two, many traditional Western psychological models completely discount the possibility for transcendent states of awareness, either by considering them pathological or relegating them to the land of outright fantasy. Freud took the former route. Presumably, traditional behaviorism takes the latter. A few Western thinkers have made laudable incursions into this dark continent of psychology. Others, including physicians, scientists, and practitioners of various disciplines, have elaborated various theories to explain the process of self-transformation and the state of enlightenment. These explanations fall into three general categories: 1) enlightenment as the next psychological stage of evolution; 2) enlightenment as making conscious the unconscious mind; and 3) enlightenment as the expression of objectless awareness. I hold that these three views are not mutually exclusive but are all valid aspects of the state of enlightenment.

A number of themes elaborated in Chapters One and Two should be echoed here. First and most importantly, there is no one state of enlightenment. Rather, there are a number of disparate though related mental states that have been grouped under that rubric. Moksha, satori, samadhi, nirvana, cosmic consciousness, and unity consciousness, to name a few, are diverse terms coming from different disciplines and cultures. But these may also be quite different states. It is only reasonable to assume that, just as different physical exercises may enhance and develop differing physical skills and abilities, so various forms of meditation will foster diverse psychological results. In his article "Meditation Research: The Evolution and State of the Art," Roger Walsh notes that psychophysiological responses differ with respect to experiments done on adepts from diverse traditions:

> Once again it should not be assumed that all practices have the same effects. Zen monks, whose practice involves a continuous open receptivity to all stimuli, displayed a continuous EEG responsiveness to a repeated sound, instead of habituating to it, as non-meditators would. However, other subjects whose practice involved an internal focusing that reduces responsiveness to environmental stimuli, failed to show any EEG responses to repeated noises (Walsh 1980, 157).

Just as the bodybuilder uses heavy weights with only a few repetitions to develop strength and lighter weights in higher repetitions to develop endurance, so differing types of mental exercise may bring increased capacities in only certain areas. One type of meditation might increase emotional stability and motivation, while another type might enhance the process of self-insight. An important area in science in the years to come will be not only to validate these states, but to outline different types of techniques with their various specific results.

The enlightenment-as-evolution theory may now be elaborated. In a general sense, the concept that transformation is an *individual* form of evolution is as old as the Vedas. But with Darwin, the term "evolution" came to have a much more specific and scientifically delineable meaning. "Evolution of the species" has been associated with materialism and humanism—the potent modern philosophies that have characteristically rejected the transcendent. In what was perhaps the first serious attempt to place superconscious mental states in a Darwinian context, however, the physician Richard M. Bucke published his book *Cosmic Consciousness.* Bucke's view, most simply, was that if evolution has brought self-conscious humankind this far, the chances are great that evolution is still at work, slowly transforming contemporary man into something superhuman. As such, we are still evolving *as a species.* In all evolutionary development, there must be a few individuals in the vanguard: the first few creatures to crawl from the sea, the first anthropoid apes to stand upright, and perhaps within the last million years, the first to have vestiges of self-consciousness. Similarly, argues Bucke, the so-called "mystical interlude"—characterized by a break with normal subject/object consciousness, with its long-lasting effects on behavior and psychological outlook—is an adumbration of what will be the status quo for the superhumanity of the future.

No scientist doubts that evolution has produced great cognitive and psychological effects, as well as physical changes in the hierarchy of species. If they once occurred, it seems reasonable to believe that psychological changes are still occurring. Bucke argues that simple consciousness—characterized by stimulus-response functioning in lower forms of life—is to self-consciousness as self-consciousness is to cosmic consciousness. The modern mystic is evolutionarily ahead of his time; today's brief interludes of cosmic consciousness are tomorrow's everyday level. Bucke goes on to argue that the greatest spiritual personages of history—e.g., the Buddha, Christ, Lao Tzu, St. Paul, St. John of the Cross—are really simply examples of what man will be at the next evolutionary stage.

Of course, Bucke's analysis does not really comport with Darwinian evolution in its more specific aspects. Bucke would be hard pressed to delineate how chance variation and natural selection could account for evolution when many of the greatest sages have not themselves produced offspring. Further, it might be argued that it is difficult to see the survival value of love, openness, and humility in a world such as ours in which a premium is put on aggressiveness and hostility. As William James wrote with his characteristic wit, "It must be confessed that, as far as the world goes, anyone who makes a saint out of himself does so at his own peril." On the other hand, it is no news that chance variation and natural selection are no longer defensible as the means by which physical evolution occurs, and that modern paleontologists and geneticists are frantically groping for a new model. It is also arguable that the qualities of the sage do have survival value on a worldwide basis: e.g., aggression can have catastrophic effects in a world that has at its disposal the nuclear arsenal with which to vent it.

This is not the place to rehash either the evolution-creation debate or the equally burning controversy in contemporary science over which particular form of evolution to accept. Instead, we have examined the attempt to reconcile the prevalence of transrational mental states with a nonreductionistic brand of evolution. As long as the model of evolution is itself in question, it seems best to simply point to the commonsense probability that evolution is an on-going process, and that it is at least conceivable that its next stage could be manifesting in transrational states. Further, insofar as man is to a great extent the director of his own development, man can choose his own goal. Evolution ceases to be entirely deterministic to the extent that man can envision the prototype for future man, and then take the necessary steps, individually and socially, to realize his vision. This is indeed an exciting prospect.

The second major theory to explain enlightenment holds that the subject obliterates the barrier between conscious and unconscious, effectively making conscious everything that was once unconscious. Ken Wilber posits just such a view:

> Development—or evolution—consists of a series of hierarchical transformations or *unfoldings* of the deep structures out of the ground-unconscious, starting with the lower (body) and ending with the highest (God). When—and *if*—all of the ground-unconscious has emerged, then there is *only* consciousness—all is conscious *as* the All. As Aristotle put it, when all potential has been actualized, the result is God (Wilbur 1980, 107).

Huston Smith has elucidated a similar account of what enlightenment is: "An enlightened being, I am proposing, is one who is in touch with his deepest unconscious which . . . deserves to be considered sacred" (Smith 1982, 179).

Other versions of this account abound. In *Yoga and Psychoanalysis*, physician Rudolph Ballentine draws a number of compelling parallels between Western psychotherapy and Eastern spiritual disciplines. The process of psychoanalysis is compared to the training of the young *sisya* or student. Ultimately, the goals are similar, though Eastern psychology presumably takes the process to its logical extreme. Whereas Western psychoanalysis attempts to uncover the unconscious motivational factors in neurotic or psychotic behavior with the cure coming through the knowledge of these previously recondite forces, yoga attempts to illuminate the unconscious mind completely. Self-knowledge means knowledge of the *entire* self—and the entire self includes the realm of the unconscious (Ballentine 1976).

Numerous other writers have elaborated similar notions throughout history. The pre-Freudian rationalists Fichte, Schelling, and Helgel have themes that resonate with the concern for transcendence and its place in evolution. But the tide of Western philosophy was to turn, with renewed popularity of positivism and with the demand for empirical verification. Positivists discounted the notion of the unconscious mind as beyond empirical demonstration. Still other currents, running deep in the history of philosophy, also inveighed against the concept of the unconscious. Though he was no empiricist, Descartes greatly influenced Western philosophy with his all-encompassing dichotomy between mind and body. For Descartes, that which is conscious *is* the mind. Everything else is material, matter. There is nothing left for an intermediate realm that is mental and yet unconscious. How could something be mental, Descartes would have argued, if it is not readily knowable, ponderable, or fathomable by the conscious mind? Because of this very compelling influence in Western thought, many who posited the existence of the unconscious were induced to argue that this term is shorthand for *physical* drives which may have behavioral results.

The solution to the Cartesian dilemma is relatively straightforward. Basically, there are many brain processes occurring at any given time, only some of which correspond to conscious thought. The remaining processes are still "mental," though they are not at the time conscious. Nevertheless, they can have behavioral effects; they can affect those brain processes that are conscious; and they may themselves become conscious at a later time. If it were possible to eliminate awareness of those processes of which we *are* readily conscious, then awareness of these other "low-intensity" neural processes might become possible. If we view consciousness as a "threshold"—a relationship between the overall pattern of brain functioning that determines alertness and the specific objects of that alertness—then it seems that lowering that threshold can occur by screening out the more powerful thoughts. Attention may then be focused on subtler processes, including those that were once *un*conscious. Indeed, this is exactly the process by which many forms of meditation operate.

The eventual goal of all these processes is enlightenment. And if enlightenment can be defined as that state wherein the subject may at will become aware of the most refined levels of thought—or beyond—then he has indeed made the unconscious conscious. In so doing, he has opened up the entire personality. The result, behaviorally and subjectively, is a state of deep insight and profound equanimity.

It makes no philosophical waves to conjecture that introspection may move to subtle mental processes. Every major philosopher, rationalist or empiricist, has written of introspection. However, the notion of going *beyond* thought would be challenged by most twentieth-century philosophers and psychologists. Western thought has made the distinction between awareness and the object *of* awareness, maintaining that the former cannot exist without the latter. It was Franz Brentano who made objects of awareness the sine qua non of awareness itself. Put simply, to be aware is to be aware *of something.* In this context the concept of pure awareness—consciousness without an object—is as self-contradictory as philosophy's proverbial married bachelor.

Apparently, Plotinus had not read Brentano when he wrote that the mind upon meditation "will arrive not at another thing, but at itself." The literature of the past from East and West is replete with similar accounts. But perhaps it is best to hear it from a contemporary writer, in case older accounts are viewed as the product of some great historical pathology. The modern-day mystic Franklin Merrell-Wolff eloquently describes the subjective principle:

> The inner core of the 'I,' like Nirvana, is not the objective existence but is, rather, the "thread" upon which the objective material of consciousness is strung. Relative consciousness deals with the objective material but never finds the "thread" as an object. Yet it is that thread which renders all else possible. In fact, it is the most immediate and ever-present reality of all (Merrell-Wolff 1973b, 31).

The experience of pure consciousness has been described as a "steady state," a "clear channel," which revitalizes the mind and is of incredible therapeutic value. Of course, it seems physically impossible to remain at this level since it entails a complete cessation of thought. Since some thought is necessary to carry out even the most basic functions, pure consciousness cannot itself become the only mode of everyday life. Still, the ability to move to this level of experience at will is instrumental in bringing quietude and vitality to moments when one is not meditating. Thus, the effect of meditation and the experience of pure consciousness spread beyond the time of meditation to the rest of one's life. Enlightenment, then, is the state characterized, among other things, by the ability to transcend relative thought. (A description of the experience by W. T. Stace can be found in Chapter Two.)

Three Theories Compared

These three general views commonly put forward to explain what happens when one becomes enlightened in no way exhaust the description—subjective, physiological, or behavioral—of enlightenment. They are simply important focal points for respective views. But is it possible to reconcile these three, or must they remain distinct? I believe all three theories point to aspects of the same process and, as such, are complementary.

Enlightenment may be explainable as the latest stage of evolution, while the cleansing of the unconscious and the experience of objectless consciousness are the means by which this development occurs. It is irrelevant that what we here call "evolution" is ultimately furthered by individual behavior, as in the practice of meditation, as opposed to being a natural and automatic response of the organism to the environment. Many forms of adaptation and development in the descendants of humankind have occurred as a result of behavioral modifications on the part of select individuals within a species. The ability of *Homo Erectus* to stand upright and to employ his developing hands in a variety of tasks arose from behavioral responses to specific environmental factors, and this had a profound effect on the subsequent course of evolution. The development of various psycho-spiritual technologies, including meditation, yoga, and biofeedback, may be a similar response. In this manner, man takes part in directing his own evolution. Further, insofar as he is the first species to be able actually to understand alternative goals and choose paths corresponding to those ends, he not only helps bring about evolution but determines its ultimate aim.

The "pure consciousness" theory is also reconcilable with that of making the unconscious conscious. If the mind can be pictured as a spectrum of brain processes from very high intensity, which are conscious, to the very low intensity, which are unconscious, becoming aware is then a function of lowering the "threshold" of consciousness. As the high-intensity thoughts are cleared from the mind, we become aware of the lower-intensity, previously unconscious mental processes. If this threshold of awareness is lowered even further, we can imagine a level where even the lowest-intensity brain processes are screened out of awareness. At this point there is awareness without an object. This would be the level at which the mystics experience what they have confusingly called "Self," misleading the uninitiated into believing that this must be similar to other levels of self, only more fundamental. If I may be allowed to pirate Hegel's metaphor, adapting it to a slightly different context, I would describe the levels of the mind as an onion. Layer after layer can be peeled away, until at last we come to nothing. There is no center, no core of experience. And yet it is this "nothing" that is so fundamental to self-transformation.

Thus, the three theories of enlightenment may be seen as different aspects of one process. Evolution spurs itself on by driving the personality to disclose itself at its most fundamental level. In so doing, a continuum is traversed which includes all the various levels and gradations of the mind, conscious and unconscious. In the course of this explanation, I have utilized a number of metaphors in an attempt to elicit and convey the fundamental nature of self-transformation, for example, the "threshold" of awareness. However, these are potentially misleading pictures of what happens in the drive to enlightenment. I am convinced that the process must work something like I have described. But in the end, we must exhort science to fill out the explanation. Only then can the most significant questions of human personality at its farthest reaches be answered.

Being Man: In Search of the Self.

It has been written that in the English language there are at least forty different everyday definitions for the words "consciousness," "subject," and "self." Add to these the plethora of scientific or psychological definitions, each emanating from different theorists, and the situation becomes thoroughly confusing (see Chapter Two). Part of the problem, of course, is with our language. There simply are not enough different terms in English to differentiate the various types of mental processes from one another. The problem is evident even in the works of some of the greatest Western philosophers. John Locke and David Hume, among others, use the words "idea" and "impression" in equivocal and confusing ways. Sanskrit scholars have written that that language has more terms to differentiate soul, mind, and the v rious objects, activities, and processes of the mind than English, French, German, and Latin combined. This comes as no surprise when it is remembered that Indian culture, through subjective experimentation by endless generations, has evolved the elaborate systems of thought evident in the *Upanishads,* the *Bhagavad Gita,* the writings of Shankara and others.

It is readily seen how difficult it is to answer the question of selfhood. People answer the same question, Is there a "self"? in diverse ways precisely because there is an on-going process of reckless equivocation on the concept of "self" (see Chapter One, the section on "Self, Soul, and Atman"). For some, the self is that element of the personality that lives on after death. Within this group are those who believe a conscious personality survives the body, and others who posit some nonconscious life principle. The major religions are the chief exponents of the former view. A number of idealists, including Plato and the yogic philosophers, held the latter view. Others, primarily from modern philosophy and psychology, define the self as some component of mental functioning —conscious, unconscious, or both—which is not immortal and which is indirectly but subjectively experienced when one is "conscious." But even within this group there are tremendous differences.

For some the self is the complex of identifications that

one integrates into the personality. For others it is one or another set of mental processes, talents, and capacities that motivate and illuminate inner life. For still others all of these are too objective to be the self: even an innate capacity can be lost, and yet there is still a sense of identity, of I-ness. For these theorists selfhood is nothing but the result of memory; it is a relation between experiences, in which one experience is remembered in the context of another experience. The contemporary Australian philosopher D.M. Armstrong has rendered an interesting philosophical analysis along these lines. Take away the function of memory and the subject lives forever in the present, a series of disconnected phenomenal experiences.

Finally, there are some who would argue that even this is not fundamental enough. Even to the being who is devoid of memory, there is an immediacy of experience. The feeling of pain, for example, would be just as acute to the memoryless being as to ordinary self-conscious man. There is thus a feeling of pain at each present moment and, though these moments may not be temporally connected by memory, nonetheless there is a subjective feeling at each instance. It is, thus, subjective awareness that constitutes the self for the latter contingent—to be is to be aware.

Here, I will cut through all of these semantic problems by acknowledging some truth in each view, and by noting that all of these processes exist and contribute to what one calls the "self," though diverse theories may emphasize one or another of these mental functions. The feeling of selfhood is a product of the layering of all these various levels, functions, and processes. The memoryless individual has the primary sense of self that comes with bare awareness. Add a memory, and experience takes on greater dimensions. Add still other capacities such as cognition, and still another world opens up to the subject.

What is the self? The answer, basically, is that "self" is a psychological concept, experienced differently with the addition or subtraction of different mental functions *and* with varying levels of development. Thus, it is a relative phenomenon in the sense that *what the subject takes to be the self* is different at each level of development. In Chapter Four and Five it was said that Having man and Doing man experience the self as a labile, evanescent, and vulnerable entity. This is because the process of self-identification at these levels is, as Sartre called it, "a sheer activity transcending toward objects" and "a great emptiness, a wind blowing toward objects." Though neither type *physically* identifies with the object of identification—the new car, the house, the trip to Europe—still there is a powerful *psychological* identification in that each of these things infuses meaning and a sense of self-worth and direction into the life of the subject.

When we say the self is somehow dependent on the objects with which it identifies, this obviously does not mean that one disappears as an entity when the objects are destroyed. Rather, one's personality may be threatened by the loss. This loss of orientation may have grave psychological and ultimately even physical effects. Further, even if the mode of identification is not challenged, a great deal of time and energy is spent "propping up" the object or lifestyle pattern to which one is attached. In this way, the subject cuts himself off from other things and experiences which do not fit into the pattern. Or, finally, the individual spends more time trying to own the object or integrate the experience than he does simply enjoying life. Thus, identification takes an onerous toll in a number of ways.

All of this radically changes at the level of Being. Instead of the typical object and experience identification, Being man has freed himself of its paralyzing and enervating effects. The subject no longer identifies with tangible things; thus, he is not psychologically dependent on the capricious happenings of the external world. Similarly, he no longer finds self-identity in what he does or experiences. He can become, in the words of Plotinus, "established in quiet and solitary union, not at all deviating from his own essence, nor revolving about himself, but being entirely stable and becoming, as it were, stability itself."

For Being man, *self*-identification comes simply from awareness. It is not the *content* of the experience that is important but rather pure experience itself; it is not *what* he does, but *that* he does that fills his life with joy and equanimity. External happenings are of reduced significance because it simply does not matter which set of events transpires. Being man is equally at ease in all situations. Of course, there is still a basic level of needs to be fulfilled from the outside. Nourishment, light, air, and water are still essential. But the literature is replete with examples that demonstrate the adept has a great degree of control over even these physical needs. Thus, there is no need-fixation at all.

Finally, Being man has found the most profound sense of meaning in life. He has transcended even Nietzsche's notion that "he who has a why to live can bear with almost any how." Insofar as the search for meaning in life has traditionally occurred in the external world, "why" refers to something *outside* oneself which one finds, internalizes, and which brings meaning. Being man does not need a why because existence is its own highest reward, as naked existence reveals itself in its most splendid form. To him the meaning of life is as self-evident as the questions of the existentialists are absurd. Meaning is not found in some objective phenomenon, axiom, or aphorism. It is not a certain pattern of living or a particular enjoyment. In the words of Meister Eckhart:

> The most powerful prayer is a free mind and ultimately the most powerful to obtain all things, and the worthiest work of all is a free mind. . . . What is a free mind? A free mind is one that is not confused by anything or bound to anything. It has not attached its advantage to any way of life, nor does it consider its own advantage in any respect.

There is an interesting parallel between the search for meaning, contemporary style, and many people's notion of morality. In both, there is a seeking for a reason to do good and a reason for meaning *outside* oneself. Just as deep existential satisfaction cannot be rooted "out there" —outside of the self—so any attempt at deriving some moral imperative from objective principles is doomed to failure. The motivation for any act of goodness that is external to the self is suspect. For example, all reasonable minds should agree that a person who performs a "good" or helpful act because he believes he will be rewarded for it is not, strictly speaking, doing "good." The results of the act may be socially beneficial, worthy of encouragement, and may even present an example for emulation. But if the motive for the act is the desire for some reward—money, praise, or even gaining heaven or avoiding hell—then the act was not performed in goodness. Sartre's statement that "without God anything is permissible" is typical of this sentiment. Good performed for any external reason may be good in a utilitarian sense, but it is ultimately inferior to the good act performed by a free mind, simply *because* it is good.

All of the greatest philosophers and system-builders, from Plato to Kant to Mill, sought the Pegasus of objective moral justification in vain. Though their solutions differed and seemingly covered the spectrum from the a priori categorical imperative to naturalistic social utilitarianism, no theory has succeeded in truly locating an unquestionable, fundamental why of morality. Similarly, the philosophical search for meaning culminated with the existentialists, who maintain there simply is no objective meaning or, at best, it is a completely arbitrary and subjective designation for the "good life," whatever one decides that means. Modern Western culture has sustained great trepidation, morally and existentially, as a result of seeking external justification for living. We have survived the moral absolutism of an earlier age, only to attempt to replace old gods with new ones. It is high time to reject this approach along with that of nihilistic relativism, and find both meaning and morality in self-transformation.

Being man finds the locus and basis for both the good and the meaningful in *himself.* No rational justification can be given to either value, but each is simply self-evident, a byproduct of right living. This is not to say that each individual at this level will necessarily agree as to what the best alternative is in each possible situation. Being man has no more of a direct line to some absolute moral realm than he does to a metaphysical realm. However, whatever the differences of opinion might be, one thing is certain. Once Being man has determined to his own satisfaction what is right in a situation, he lives in accord with this determination, even to his own detriment. So his characteristic equanimity of mind is accompanied by moral certitude, not in the epistemological sense of always knowing what is right, but rather, in the sense that he will adhere to what he holds to be right to the best of his ability.

Returning one final time to the question, What is the "self"? it can be said that "self" is any level of conscious mental functioning. When this conscious functioning has been purged of all of the *objects* of awareness, sensory and cognitive, what emerges is the most fundamental self in the sense that it is the bedrock on which all other mental states are built. At the moment of pure awareness, not even the *quality* of awareness is given, for this would be an objective thought. It is at this moment—for reasons that will perhaps remain forever unanalyzable but simply phenomenologically given—that the subject feels more *himself* than ever before. The state is experienced as unchanging because the experience of pure awareness encompasses no flow of thought. It is experienced as beyond space because the phenomenal experience of spatial locality is a product of thought. If Kant was correct that space, time, and causation, among other concepts, do not exist objectively but are products of the organizing mind, then pure consciousness might be understood as the state that is psychologically prior to the schematizing principle of objective consciousness. This may explain similar claims of the mystics, including the perception that all is a contradiction.

In conclusion, whatever the veridical status the philosophers assign to the experience, and whatever psychological theory is forwarded to explain such states, it is undeniable that such states exist. Though the routes to them may vary from discipline to discipline, and though other paths may have evolved various end states altogether, the impact of the experience of pure awareness on a variety of people is well known.

What Good is Being Man?

In a recent popular movie the star, who had spent his life searching for himself by living in various locales and doing assorted jobs, goes to the Himalayas to learn under a great master. He lives for some time in the Tibetan wilderness, studying the *Upanishads* and listening to the ancient sage. At one point he is sent out alone into the winter snows to contemplate life and to find enlightenment. As the fire he carefully guards begins to smolder, he rips out the pages from the holy book to feed the flames. Somehow, we know he has found his goal. He returns to the monastery to prepare to leave, and is confronted by the master who tells him that he has come so close, that he should not abandon the pursuit just yet. At this, the protagonist turns to the master and says, "It must be easy to be a holy man on the top of a mountain."

The story is an old one with many versions, beginning with the tale of Zarathustra. The wisdom, however, is the same, and that wisdom holds that what one learns means nothing if it is not put to an earthly use. The seeker after enlightenment sinks to the level of the street derelict if part of his pursuit is not made for the benefit of others. There is nothing quite so worthy of contempt as the effete, self-enthralled reverie of the would-be philosopher, adept, or sage. Wisdom unused is worse than ignorance; it is a repudiation of the value of other lives, a renunciation not of self but of the other. Isolated mountains and ivory towers may be important but as places of renewal, not for permanent retreat.

Being man is not the withered ascetic or the solitary recluse who treads a lonely, lifelong circle round his own center of consciousness. He "abjures the realm" only to re-enter it, to confront the problems of the unemancipated. His brand of detachment is that of detachment from *himself*, not from others. If he rises to high places, he lends his wisdom to the formation of public policy, to the equitable distribution of justice, or to the amelioration of international tensions. But he is less a statesman than a *worlds*man, for his loyalties are to human beings, not to nations, and his patriotism is universal. If he remains among the people, he lends his wisdom and comfort to all he encounters. He is, in short, a man of action; he has combined the best of inner spiritual perfection and outward energy and commitment. Being man truly is man at his most excellent, an idealized version of all that is most humane, cultivated, and selfless in humankind.

Though ultimately the job must remain hopelessly incomplete, it has been my intention to provide a general picture of the enlightened individual. More than anything, my hope has been to place the possibility for psychospiritual development in a Western context, devoid of the metaphysical and otherworldly connotations prevalent in the West. Consequently, I have not devoted space to investigating certain claims, bordering on the supernatural, traditionally associated with the subject. Some of these claims, such as reincarnation, are in direct conflict with the naturalistic metaphysic set forth in the first two chapters. Other claims, such as clairvoyance and ESP, are beginning to be studied by academic science and must wait for some other book. I remain uncommitted on these issues.

III

Twentieth-Century Man

7
Time, Death, and the Society Without a Goal

There are many from all avenues of our culture who believe that contemporary Western society represents the last throes of a dying civilization. We have been given everything materially desirable; our lives have been lengthened by the advent of modern medicine; and our free time has been enhanced and extended by modern technology, transportation, and communications. Even our libido has been unchained from its Victorian moorings, free to drift self-indulgently about the waters of a less repressive—or perhaps simply more desultory—era. We are doomed to die out, the prophets say, in our air-conditioned cages, victims of material overabundance, overpopulation, and genuine, deep-rooted existential apathy. In the words of historian Crane Brinton:

> We cannot see ourselves as others will see us. It is one of the marks of our own time that there are probably more people than usual in Western culture since the hope-fear of the second coming of Christ faded for most men, who hold that we shall not be seen at all, our history having ended, after our prolonged whimpers, with a grand bang (Brinton 1959, 413).

In these next two chapters twentieth-century man and culture will be examined in an attempt to demonstrate that, far from the doomsday picture many paint, Western civilization may be on the brink of a great transition. We look to a renaissance in human values, world view, and the existential *raison d'être*. Before we can change ourselves, however, we must clearly know ourselves—our fears, our fetishes and our fantasies.

The Decline of Religious Commitment

While he was in prison for his pacifist activities in World War I, Bertrand Russell was asked by the jailer, as part of a survey, what his religious denomination was.

"Atheist," he replied.

"Atheist?" repeated the jailer. "Never heard of that one, but just so long as we all believe in the same God."

Atheism and agnosticism are not particularly new positions in the history of ideas. There have been a few skeptics in almost every culture, and these were often the most learned members of society. Unfortunately, because of religious oppression such thinkers were often forced to disguise their views by using the word "God" to designate anything but what most people meant by the word. Spinoza and Einstein are two examples, both of whom used "God" to designate the laws of nature.

Despite the traditional rarity of the atheist, the position has become somewhat more popular in the past century, probably a result of the growth of science and an increasing distrust of traditional organized religion and religious orthodoxy. A recent Gallup poll indicates that one in ten Americans do not believe in God, either in a personal or impersonal form. Another fifteen percent countenance only a vague, impersonal God. This loose-fitting notion may be anything from Aristotle's and Jefferson's supreme watchmaker to Spinoza's even less psychologically rewarding concept. Thus, one-quarter of the American population rejects the Judeo-Christian concept of a personally involved Supreme Being (Gallup Feb., 1984).

A second and even more interesting group surveyed

consists of the "nominal" Christian, which made up a "significant proportion" of the American population. Fifty-one percent of the American public was classified as "fairly low" or "very low" on a scale of spiritual commitment. Only twelve percent was "highly spiritually committed." An astounding forty percent of those who consider themselves "committed Christians" do not know that Christ delivered the Sermon on the Mount. A similar "significant proportion" of "Christians" do not believe in the divinity of Christ. Many from this group believe it is possible to be a "true Christian" and at the same time reject the divinity of Christ. Despite these shocking statistics, seventy percent of Americans consider themselves church members and sixty percent attend church at least once a month. Finally, a *Wall Street Journal* survey indicated that, even of those who consider themselves practicing Christians, there is little difference between the habits of the churched and the unchurched (cited in the Gallup Poll, Feb., 1984).

This evidence is significant because it indicates that a vast number of people—over half of the American public—are modern-day unbelieving believers. They are "extrinsically oriented" and find church-going, when they do it, more a means to social fellowship than to spiritual realization. This nominal affiliation affords the unbelieving believer a sense of having the traditional ties to a religious institution, along with the psychological bonus of a general religious orientation, beneficial in times of grief and stress, without requiring the commitment necessary for genuine spiritual involvement.

Western society has witnessed a decline in religious orientation, despite statistics that indicate seven in ten Americans are church-goers. This is true notwithstanding the recent fundamentalist and "born again" revivals. Western religiosity has declined not so much in number as in degree or quality of belief. Further, all indications are that this trend will continue indefinitely into the future. As a result, modern man is a metaphysical mugwump. He sits on the fence that is supposed to partition the realm of science from that of religion, swinging his cup from side to side, depending on where the momentary advantage is to be found, seeking solace in the supernatural when science has failed, but at all other times, turning his back on the moral requirements and doctrinal dictates of traditional religion. He truly is a fair-weather friend to religion, and he pays the price for it. Indeed, the unbelieving believer is haunted by a metaphysical uncertainty that sinks to the very root of his being. This insecurity makes itself known in what is perhaps the most fundamental problem of human existence—the fear of death and the desire for everlasting life. Deep-seated uncertainty becomes evident at times of confrontation with death. We are told that Mary Baker Eddy, founder of the Christian Science movement—which teaches the immorality of contravening the ways of God by use of modern medicine—called a doctor to her own deathbed. Stories like the following, all with a similar moral, are played out anew on a daily basis.

About ten years ago, the federal court judge Skelly Wright was called to the hospital room of a Jehovah's Witness. The patient had refused a blood transfusion, without which he would soon die. The judge could issue a court order to save the man's life forcibly.

"Do you want a blood transfusion?" asked Wright.

"No," the patient replied.

"Why not?"

"Because I'll be breaking one of God's highest laws if I take another's blood. I'll rot in hell forever."

"Will you rot in hell if the transfusion is given to you against your will?" asked Wright.

"No, I suppose not—if it's against my will."

"O.K.," rejoined Wright, evincing the highly honed reasoning necessary in law. "Do you want a blood transfusion given to you against your will?"

"Yes," the patient responded readily.

Apparently, even a logical contradiction is not too much to embrace when faced with eternity. What is revealing, however, is that even the "devout" readily do so. If it is true that no man who truly believes in God, with the attendant guarantee of an afterlife in one form or another, is afraid to die, then it appears that true belief is in short supply in our time. It is precisely in this hope or quest for immortality that religious belief, or lack thereof, comes home to roost with a vengeance. It is here that a man's metaphysics ceases to be an abstract matter and is acknowledged for the psychological import that it has.

The Fear of Death and the Cult of Dorian Gray

"God is dead," wrote Nietzsche. An old joke has God retorting, "Nietzsche is dead." It is from our repudiation of the divine that we derive our fear of death. And it is this dread for our own mortality that precipitates modern man's ambivalent relationship with time.

Ours is a truly paradoxical existence, for we are engaged in a love-hate relationship with time. We can see just how paradoxical this relationship is by asking ourselves at the close of any day whether, knowing what we know now, we would care to live this day over again to the last detail. I do not believe it presumptuous to assume that, for most people on most days, the answer would be no. Even if we could erase the memory of today so as to eliminate the mundaneness of repetition, most people on most days would not want to live today again tomorrow. Indeed, it is a great enigma that generally we eagerly await the end of the day, the passing of the week, or the end of the year, recklessly casting todays aside like counterfeit bills, hoping for tomorrows—until they arrive—waiting for time to pass and, at the same time, literally living in mortal fear of death, the end of the long string of todays.

Modern man lives an ironic existence. The consumption of experience and the living of life in all its aspects require the passing of time, yet with each passing day there is the knowledge that we are one day closer to death. It is as if we pay for each happiness with a small bit of the finite supply of time allotted to each of us. And when that finite supply is exhausted, death is the last reward. It is ultimately our fear of death that precipitates our uncertain relationship with time. As William James has said, death is the "worm at the core" of our pretensions to happiness.

Yet modern Western man seems peculiarly afflicted with the preoccupation for, and repressive denial of, the process of aging and death. Our culture has put a premium on youth and on the luxuries that youth can afford as no society has before us. Everywhere we are besieged with media messages that exhort us to relive our youth. Photography has been subjugated to capturing "the times of your life," while everything from toothpaste to automobiles is marketed by identification with the cult of Dorian Gray, the pervasive trend characterized by the desire to remain forever young. Man has always sought to better his life and health, and the long-awaited developments that have made it all possible are an important part of our culture. But when the desire to make life healthier and longer degenerates into the useless preoccupation with disguising gray hairs, along with the variety of other superficial behaviors promulgated by advertising, then the cult of youth has overextended itself.

Perhaps the eighteenth-century philosopher Michel Montaigne saw the fundamental problem long before our time when he said, "If we have learned how to live properly and calmly, we will know how to die in the same manner." Modern man, however, has learned neither. He lives furiously and he denies death at every turn. And when he is confronted with the issue he adopts the attitude of the unbelieving believer. Bertrand Russell recounts the story of a conversation between two guests at a dinner party. The discussion turned to a debate on the prospect of human immortality. One guest asked a second what he thought would happen to him when he died. At first, the second guest simply ignored the question. The first guest persisted, repeating his question. Finally, the second guest replied, "Oh well, I suppose I shall inherit eternal bliss, but I wish you wouldn't talk about such unpleasant subjects" (Russell 1958, 107). This is characteristic of the modern metaphysical outlook. Like the ancient Medean king who was reputed to have converted to every religion just to play it safe, modern man retains the scant trappings of an ancient belief system as a psychological safeguard—or worse, a type of metaphysical "fire insurance"—never daring to think too closely about what he believes in. When his convictions are challenged, he responds not with the open-minded curiosity characteristic of one who is secure in his belief, but with the hostility, intolerance, and dogmatic rigidity that marks the fearful.

If it is true, as argued, that in the words of Lasch, "the fear of death takes on new intensity in a society that has deprived itself of religion and shows little interest in posterity," then the cult of Dorian Gray is certainly the result to be expected. Social philosopher Ernest Becker has also studied the modern reaction to death in comparison to that of primitive cultures:

> To be sure, primitives often celebrate death . . . *because* they feel that death is the final promotion, the final elevation to a higher form of life, to the enjoyment of eternity in some form. Most modern Westerners have trouble believing this any more, which is what makes the fear of death as prominent a part of our psychological make-up (Becker 1973, ix).

It is also significant that modern metaphysical uncertainty is probably the *worst* position to take in the hope of coming to terms with death. According to Panos D. Bardis, a researcher of social attitudes toward death, "Empirical research indicates that the lowest fear is found among true believers and nonbelievers in religion, while nominal believers experience the highest fear" (Bardis 1981, 5). Thus, it seems that from a psychological point of view even the sentiment of a Bertrand Russell—"When I die, I shall rot and nothing of my ego will survive"—is preferable to that of the metaphysical mugwump.

Modern man is thus in a situation which is unenviably

ironic, and he retains the outline of a belief which serves only to further the anxiety that saturates his existence. And despite his attempts at denial, he is deeply convinced of his mortality. William James depicts the plight of modern man in what is one of the most moving passages from all of philosophy:

> For naturalism, fed on recent cosmological speculations, mankind is in a position similar to that of a set of people living on a frozen lake, surrounded by cliffs over which there is no escape, yet knowing that little by little the ice is melting, and the inevitable day drawing near when the last film of it will disappear, and to be drowned ignominiously will be the human creature's portion. The merrier the skating, the warmer and more sparkling the sun by day, and the ruddier the bonfires at night, the more poignant the sadness with which one must take in the meaning of the total situation (James 1961, 124).

Lost in Time: Modern Man and Psychohistorical Dislocation

There is another significant way in which our culture manifests a fundamental conflict with time. Where the denial of death is accompanied by a *personal* metaphysical ambivalence to time, there is another sense in which we simply are not at home with time. Indeed, we are alienated from the continuity of the temporal flow. This factor is what Lifton has called "psycho-historical dislocation." It is characterized by

> . . . the break in the sense of connection which men have long felt with the vital and nurturing symbols of their cultural tradition—symbols revolving around family, idea systems, religion, and the life cycle in general. In our contemporary world one perceives these traditional symbols . . . as irrelevant, burdensome or inactivating, and yet one cannot avoid carrying them within or having one's self-process profoundly affected by them (Lifton 1970, 31).

Psycho-historical dislocation is the state in which modern man sees the future as a threatening, tumultuous, never-ending series of revolutions, social and scientific, while the past is perceived as having little significance in the contemporary world. Modern man finds himself in a temporal purgatory, having nothing to learn from the past and nothing to contribute to the future, living for the moment and for himself, not for his predecessors or for posterity.

What has precipitated this alienation from the past and ambivalence toward the future? Some of the factors have already been discussed. We fear the future because we fear death, because we have lost our hope for immortality and belief in the transcendent. The future, however, is lost to us in other ways as well.

The historian Crane Brinton has delineated three senses in which we have attempted to secure an extension of ourselves beyond the grave: personal immortality, immortality through propagation, and immortality through works (Brinton, 1959). Having largely lost genuine faith in a personal afterlife, we as a society have attempted to restore a sense of immortality in other ways. Immortality through propagation, a pale surrogate for the real thing, seems first to have been embraced by the Jews of the Old Testament. To live on through our children is to countenance cultural, if not personal, immortality. As such, the individual may take some stock in the future, even if he will not be there personally to witness the result.

This substitute is of little reward in an age like ours, when growing numbers of people believe the world as we know it will end in nuclear destruction within a generation. According to a recent Gallup poll, international strife and fear of nuclear war was *the most important* problem on the collective mind of the American public (Gallup April 1985). According to another poll, thirty-three percent of the nation thought that World War III was more than likely to occur within the next ten years. Another nineteen percent thought there was a fifty-fifty chance of this occurring. Perhaps even more interesting was the finding that fear of nuclear annihilation was greatest among the younger age groups, with a corresponding decline in "nuclear anxiety" with an increase in age (Gallup Feb. 1985). This may indicate that it is the young who have the greatest feeling of futurelessness. The hope for cultural, if not personal, immortality by propagation is dampened by the public perception that the world as we know it simply will not exist in the near future. For some the very prospect of bringing children into this world is rejected.

Beyond the specter of mutually assured destruction looms yet another set of cultural factors contributing to the sense of a lost connection with the future. The advent of what Toffler calls "throw-away society" and the "economics of impermanence" are partially the result of a culture that leaves little intact from one generation to the next. Indeed, it can even be questioned whether the word "culture"—meaning an enduring system of traditions and institutions—is applicable in the modern era. This will be discussed at some length shortly.

Immortality by works has also been undercut in the last century. The work ethic—which was as much a sign that the old supernatural world view was crumbling as it was an attempt to replace it—was the socioeconomic manifestation of the hope for immortality through works. The notion that a good material life with its blessings of progress and prosperity comes with old-fashioned hard work produced a changing concept of man's relationship to God. By this view, God's work was to be done by man, and the subduing of nature for the betterment of man was the first step in the furthering of the Word. Economic prosperity was thoroughly connected with hopes of otherworldly grace.

As modern man relinquished his fading hope for an afterlife, however, work became an end in itself. This end has become something of a mania in the late twentieth century, when many not only live to work but completely define themselves in terms of their profession. Brinton has called this the competing for the *agun* and Robin Williams, social critic, has written that "American Society is marked by a central stress upon personal achievement. The success story and the respect accorded to the self-made man are distinctly American if they are anything" (Lasch 1979, 105).

Even this pallid attempt at "leaving a little part of oneself" behind in the world, however, is increasingly futile. The trend of mushrooming professional specialization, along with the accelerated rate of turnover of information, has rendered improbable the prospect of leaving behind anything enduring. In the sciences and technology, advances made today will probably be rendered totally obsolete in just a few years. In art, music, and literature, tastes and fashions seem to change so dramatically in such a short time—as a result of the frenetic search for novelty—that current trends promise to be nothing more than counterpoint to some previous trend, becoming the touchstone to which some equally ephemeral later trend may react. In many areas of professional life, the work ethic may survive as a route to personal orientation and psychological integration, but not as a means of leaving something of oneself to the future. The probability is great that, because of the explosion of technology, posterity will do to us as we have done to our own past.

Modern man is lost in time because he has, personally and culturally, lost faith in the future, and because he has abjured his past. It seems, as Lukacs has written, that "God and history seem to have died together." If a sense of psychological, cultural, and historical continuity is essential to the rejuvenation of "post-modern" man, then it seems that a new paradigm by which to gauge human progress is essential. All of the old temporal measuring-sticks have been rendered either thoroughly obsolete or hopelessly inadequate. Human progress, measured in terms of otherworldly grace, material prosperity, or technological innovation—all of which have been woefully inadequate in capturing the essence of man's nature and his current place in history—must give way to a new concept of what it means to be human. With this new guiding image, man will regain his place in history or, perhaps more accurately, he will find that he has not lost it.

The Society Without a Goal

Central to the analyses of many social critics is the contention that contemporary culture has lost its sense of purpose and direction. According to this view, we as a society have satisfied most of the long-strived-for goals, political and economic, only to find that there is nothing left for which to fight. We are victims of our own wealth, cultural plurality, and social "egalitarianism." Apathy and mediocrity have claimed the final victory, they argue. In one important sense they are correct. Eric Hoffer, the longshoreman turned philosopher and spokesman for the middle class, has written, "We are beginning to suspect that to fulfill a hope is to defeat it, and to make a dream come true is to turn it into a nightmare" (Hoffer 1976).

If social criticism could be written like a bad novel, twentieth-century man would be the tragic hero of a story that would begin, "He had it all," and then recount the subsequent fall of this hero. In an age when for the first time in history the majority of American children can no longer expect to rise above their father's station in life, professionally and economically, modern man's sense of direction has been swept from beneath him. In the words of Lukacs, "Life is becoming, life is the wish for more life, life is worth living when we have something to look forward to, life involves aspiration. . . . When the sense of some these aspirations disappears, [people] are alone and bewildered" (Lukacs 1970, 78). Hoffer maintains that, "One of the lessons of the 1960s has been that abundance, freedom, equality, and justice are not the most fundamental ingredients of a satisfactory existence." If this is the case, what *is* the more fundamental ingredient?

The criticism that modern society is without a goal is

only partially accurate. If these claims are taken to mean that modern people, particularly the younger generation, are now without a goal to which to apply themselves and to which to devote their existence, then the complaint is well taken. It is absolutely essential to recognize this as a basic fact of twentieth-century life. If, on the other hand, the claim of directionlessness is interpreted to mean that contemporary man *wants* no goal, seeking rather to live a desultory existence with no specific aspiration, then the claim could not be further from the truth. From the standpoint of the past, the change in values and search for a new direction in life appears to be something of a transgression. But from the paradigmatic standpoint of the future, this search will be recognized as a *transcendence*. To fulfill a hope is not to defeat it; it is to evolve a new and higher hope. We are only now beginning to recognize in what direction this hope, this goal, and this ideal lie.

Some Thoughts on the Cure for Twentieth-Century Man

If societies as well as individuals can be sick, and if twentieth-century culture truly is sick as many have suggested, then what if anything is the cure? Correctly speaking, modern man is not sick in any traditional sense of the word. Instead, his malady is developmental rather than regressive; it is more akin to a "growing pain" than to a degenerative ailment.

Essentially, modern man suffers from being "between stages," psycho-spiritually speaking. He has relinquished his old pleasures but has found no new ones to replace them. He has largely achieved his old goals—materially, socially, and politically—and is yet to discover the new set of aspirations toward which he can devote his life, and which will give life meaning. He has satisfied a whole spectrum of lower needs and exhibits a surplus of energy that has not yet been applied to the next stage—a new, hierarchically emergent level of needs. Perhaps fundamentally he has grown weary of an old lifestyle and seeks to construct a new one. Indeed, he seeks to develop a new sense of self.

The road to a new life consists basically in gratefully accepting those things without which development would have been impossible, but not *defining* ourselves in terms of them. Economic self-sufficiency is essential, but is rather a necessary than a sufficient condition to a satisfactory existence. Social and political equality are absolutely fundamental in order to foster the physical, psychological, and spiritual development of the less fortunate. (A great deal remains to be done here. In Third World countries the process which has recently culminated for greater America has only just begun.) Further, we must remain vigilant to jealously protect these political and socioeconomic conditions—a free society is essential to further psycho-spiritual development. But we must go further than all this. We must recognize a higher potential in man and begin to develop it. In the following paragraphs I offer some general thoughts on how this development could be fostered, individually and ideologically.

First, it is essential that the concept of *progress* take a new form. Despite the contention of at least one historian who claims that the notion of progress became important in the minds of common men only three or four centuries ago, the idea seems almost innate in man. Though it has been defined in different ways, this concept has powered the great religions and metaphysical systems from the beginning of recorded history—from the Hindu-Buddhist conception of repeated rebirth until salvation and release from the process, to the Christian eschatology ending in the Second Coming and Judgment Day.

As already elaborated, the last few centuries have witnessed a change in the conception of progress from metaphysical to socioeconomic. Progress on the cultural level became a function of economic or technological development, while personal progress was gauged in financial or occupational advancement. The modern worker views life as a process of accumulating wealth or cultivating occupational advancement. This is all that is left of the once-powerful concept. Now even this situation is no longer satisfactory, personally or culturally.

In place of technological or financial progress, modern man must begin to orient his life around a psycho-spiritual vision of progress. Life should be lived not just to accumulate money, but to accumulate wisdom, not to develop a stock portfolio, but to develop oneself. Love and humor, not despair and cynicism, should mark his life.

To date, a psycho-spiritual form of progress has simply been overlooked or ignored by Western civilization, and for a variety of reasons. First, it has not been viewed as a real possibility. The notion that individually "man does not get better, he only gets old" has been prevalent. Further, any advances as a culture have been attributed to scientific advances, more than to any transcendental moral development. On a more practical level, we have been preoccupied with lower, developmentally prior technological and socioeconomic advances. Despite these reasons, the tide has begun to turn. Western man is beginning to envision the possibility of psycho-spiritual development.

A new vision of progress, along with a new view of self, will grant man a new sense of history, reuniting him with his past and future. When progress is viewed in technological terms, the present is little like the past and even less like the future. But when history is viewed as a series of challenges, goals, achievements, and new challenges—all of which are leading to the psycho-spiritual realization of man—alienation from our past becomes psycho-historical integration as we come to realize a goal more comprehensive than all previous goals.

A new image of man, with a corresponding sense of progress and of goal in life, will serve to reorient man historically, to give him a new sense of purpose and, most importantly, literally to foster the evolution of consciousness, culturally and individually.

8
The Withering of Eden?

The demise of modern Western civilization is forecast by a sizable contingent of historians, philosophers, and social critics. These doomsayers point to a number of social and psychological trends, such as fragmentation and the escalating use of drugs, which threaten to destroy the very foundation of our culture. However, there is another way to look at these trends, troublesome as they are. I will argue that, rather than spelling disaster, these seemingly negative aspects of our society are expressions of the imperative for personal and cultural transformation. They are the progeny of a misdirected search for self-transcendence, both socially and individually, a headlong cultural search which heralds a new age and a new ideal for man.

Freedom and Fragmentation

Some years ago, a professor of philosophy I know walked into an ice cream parlor that boasted seventy-five different flavors. He had come in for a vanilla cone. Upon entering, he was overwhelmed by the selection, which included everything from pumpkin to banana fudge to bubble-gum flavored ice cream. Paralyzed by the variety, he might have been heard to echo the words of Hegel that anything taken to an extreme, even freedom, tends to negate itself. After some minutes of confused deliberation he left—clutching the vanilla cone for which he had originally come.

Though this situation is a simple one, with equivalents that occur all over the modern world every day, nonetheless, there is a powerful dialectic at work. If the proliferation of choice in consumer products, lifestyles, friends, roles, heroes, entertainments can be considered a type of freedom, then in a sense modern man is more *free* than any before him. This freedom of choice is a significant, even overwhelming, reality in everyday life, as is evident to anyone who has traversed the aisles of a supermarket. This kind of freedom has permeated every corner of our culture and every area of modern life.

Such freedom is made possible by the ever-escalating cycle of consumer-directed technology and peddled by increasingly subtle and sophisticated marketing techniques. Over fifteen years ago, Toffler graphically documented the trend as a function of a combination of competition, diversification, and the "planned obsolescence" of products (Toffler 1970, 303-327). By all accounts, the trend has only gained impetus since that time.

Another area where diversity is particularly evident is in modern education. Lasch, among others, describes the consumerization of education (Lasch 1979, 221-266). A century ago John Cardinal Newman saw the beginning of a trend that has reached incredible proportions today:

> [Education has made] the error of distracting and enfeebling the mind with an unending profusion of subjects, implying that a smattering in a dozen branches of study is not shallowness. . . . What the steam engine does with matter, the printing press is to do with the mind; it is to act mechanically, and the population is to be passively, almost unconsciously enlightened by the mere multiplication and dissemination of volumes (Newman 1970, 379).

This trend in education reaches back into the deep past; it is not particular to our time. But only in this century have diversification and, perhaps more importantly, balkanization or compartmentalization into distinct fields of study, occurred.

In a variety of other spheres of activity, modern man is confronted with more choices than any generation before him. We easily know a dozen times as many people as our eighteenth-century ancestors did. We must choose our friends, lovers, and to some extent professional acquaintances from a correspondingly larger group of people. Sociologists today tell us that the dimensions of the average relationship have contracted, being shorter and shallower than in previous times, but there are now more of them. Because of improved transportation and communications, we have a choice of places to visit, to work, and to live on a scale hitherto unimagined. In most arenas of modern life, the same situation prevails. We are, as a culture and as individuals, literally inundated with possibilities.

Many futurists and prophets of the Orwellian strain have written of the banality, repetitiveness, and agonizing monotony of the years ahead. According to this view, soul-withering conformity, bureaucratic centralization, and social-economic interdependence will crush all spontaneity and creativity from the lives of the next generations. As it turns out, however, their predictions could not be further from the truth. Man of the future will not be crushed into conformity, as many have predicted. Quite to the contrary, "The problem, as we shall see," wrote Toffler, "is whether we can survive freedom."

In good keeping with the Hegelian tone that surfaced earlier, the proliferation of life choices in the extreme version typical of today may have quite the opposite effect. Freedom negates itself by *fragmenting* the individual, paralyzing him with the possibilities. Each act, insofar as it embodies the making of a decision or choice, comes to represent not so much an *act* as an *omission.* For everything we choose, where only one choice can be made, we are haunted by our renunciation of all the other possibilities. In this manner, life becomes not so much a celebration of *what is* as a remembrance of *what might have been.* Or, on the other hand, where no one choice is ever made, where no decision is adhered to, and where many possibilities are superficially tasted, life becomes a charade, a parade of da-glo painted faces, like the hippies, introduced in quick succession, each with a separate story to tell and no time to tell it. We are, of course, speaking of Doing man.

The forces of fragmentation have three readily identifiable manifestations at the psychological level. The first is an amorphous sense of disbelief in life, a blurring of the distinction between reality and unreality. Modern-day heroes portray this quality in a variety of ways. From the detached cynicism of the modern T.V. private detective to the "absurd man" of literature, shaking his fist at an uncaring cosmos, the underlying sense of boredom, apathy, and incredulousness are everywhere the same.

Fragmentation contributes to a sense of disbelief because there are literally so many things going on, so *many* possible choices to be made, that one feels "this can't *all* be real." The logic of the position is compelling. From the major premise that not every choice of lifestyle, vocation, religion, etc., is valid, to the minor premise that each choice is as legitimate as the next—the inevitable conclusion is that *no* choice is real, valid, or legitimate. As in modern moral relativism, the subjectivist doctrine that each choice is as valid as any other degenerates into outright iconoclastic nihilism.

In other important realms of human interaction, the same process that converts fragmentation into ubiquitous disbelief is at work. In religion, familiarity with a variety of spiritual orientations often leads to rejection of religion in general. (This fact is credited as the chief catalyst in the development of ancient Greek philosophy—a reaction to the spate of gods worshipped in the various cultures the Greeks came in contact with.)

Similar situations are found in modern politics, ethics, and other areas. With respect to the spoken word, perhaps the most fundamental ingredient of social cohesion, philosopher Philip Phenix has written, "Modern man has become cynical about language. Flooded by a ceaseless outpouring of symbols through the mass media of communication, language has tended to become a debased currency with little relation to real values and ineffective in the creation of genuine community" (Phenix 1964, 137). In all of these respects, disbelief is the irreconcilable result of cultural diversity and personal fragmentation.

A second result of the proliferation of choices is the absence of a feeling of security in the established order. In fact, not only is *the* established order challenged, the possibility for *any* order is rejected. Part of the reason for this is apparent. As social institutions which have endured for centuries disintegrate in the course of just a few decades, people naturally begin to distrust not just these particular institutions, but institutions *sui generis*. As interpersonal relationships become shallower and decrease in duration, the individual learns to orient himself so as not to become deeply attached to or involved with anybody. Similarly, the route follows from a "bad marriage" to "marriage is bad." As particular manifestations of order crumble in the revolutionary process of radical social transformation, order itself is challenged and discounted.

The third psychological symptom of modern freedom and fragmentation, intimately related to the second, is the pervasive sense that the world is entirely chaotic, random, and without any overarching significance. The modern existential rejection of order in the world is a recent philosophical expression of this. Camus' absurd man who wants nothing more than to find meaning in life must settle for calling off the search and proudly proclaiming his meaningless defiance to an equally meaningless world.

Interestingly, social historian and philosopher Thomas Kuhn, in *The Structure of Scientific Revolutions,* elaborates a number of symptoms in science, similar to those of contemporary man, that occur when the established order has been challenged or rejected. Modern man is "between paradigms," psychologically speaking. As we saw with Doing man, fragmentation can come to an end only with integration, the acceptance of a new world order, and the adoption of a new image of man. Only then will a genuine sense of freedom be realized, individually and for society.

Experience as a Replacement for Possession

Perhaps one of the most powerful trends in twentieth-century culture can be best characterized as experience replacing possession as a dominant mode of modern personal orientation. The deep-seated tendency for people to seek out, accumulate, and *identify with,* experiences, not material possessions, is a natural outgrowth of the acquisitive imperative. For Doing man, "What counts is not the best living, but the most living," as Camus wrote. But how does this situation arise, culturally and personally? How has modern man—self-confessed pilgrim en route to that media-inspired promised land of the "most living"—been so ruthlessly transformed?

Billie is an attractive, twenty-one-year-old student now living on a large midwestern campus, the daughter of wealthy New York parents. Before coming back east, she traveled around the West Coast, living the life of a nomad. Here was a bohemian existence in the spirit of Kerouac—hitchhiking, sleeping in the backs of trucks or the homes of accommodating acquaintances, often themselves on the edge of society. She shared this life with a loose-knit band of ne'er-do-wells, a group that often had to split up so that one or two could catch a ride to the next town. Often Billie would travel alone, moving from town to town and encounter to encounter, only to reunite with her friends by chance, days or weeks later. From Los

Angeles to Malibu to smaller towns in southern California, she drifted for three-and-a-half years.

In talking about her life and her friends, Billie described how various sexual orientations were the "in" thing at different ages, until these were all exhausted as authentic experiences. At that point celibacy became the thing to practice. Billie's experience-seeking friends did not perceive celibacy negatively as giving something up but as a positive state, a genuine experience unto itself which they had yet to taste.

It should not be inferred from this account that experience-seeking is something restricted to the countercultural lifestyle. A great many people in all walks of life have a similar predilection. Anything from alcohol, drugs, and fast cars to jobs, friends, and lovers may appeal to the experience-seeker.

The popularized twentieth-century philosophy that all a person *does* is all a person *is,* is the predictable result of an acquisitive society that has tired of material accumulation. Where Western man once sought to accumulate things, he now emphasizes living as a means to experience as many different situations as possible; the emphasis has gone from *having* to *doing.* Eric Hoffer has written that capitalism can create abundance but does not "know how to cope with people who are interested in the quality of life rather than a higher standard of living." The quality of life to which he refers is presumably that which cannot be owned, but the function of a wealth of experience, a treasureload of memorable moments which one cultivates.

We are worshippers of experience; the more the better. Our ambivalent preoccupation with time only contributes to this cultural switch from ownership. We enshrine moments in a variety of ways: diaries, scrapbooks, and videotapes are just some of the more mundane means of doing this. As if to memorialize his very existence, the modern consumer faithfully records his life, using the latest technology. All of this insures that what small bit of time is not being taken up with experience-seeking in the present may be used by the seeker to regale himself with that of the past. Ours is a society of voracious meat eaters, consummately involved with stripping the flesh from every one of life's situations. But why is this the case and, perhaps more importantly, where is it leading us?

We must first understand the concept of material possession, along with the function it fulfills, in order fully to understand the cult of experience. Basically, there are only two functions material possessions fill: they are "tools" or "playthings." A tool, in the broadest sense of the word, is anything that saves time or energy in accomplishing daily tasks. Everything from so-called labor saving devices—washers, dryers, toasters, sewing machines—to the larger industrial machines are to be considered tools. Even a giant nuclear reactor is simply a device to save us, as a society, a certain amount of time and energy. (If a particular tool fails in its proposed function, it may not be *worth* the time and energy required to build, maintain, or acquire it.) Tools, then, are those things that are possessed to provide the owner with more free time *or* more energy with which to fill the free time.

All other material possessions are "playthings," things that we use to fill free time in a variety of pleasurable or convenient ways. The T.V. set, the stereo, books, even people may be playthings. It is, of course, possible that something can be both a tool and a plaything. For example, the family car may serve both to get the driver to and from work more efficiently, thus qualifying as a tool, while being used at other times to take rides into the country. Further, even those things that are not, strictly speaking, "used" for anything but only serve as souvenirs or status symbols—a wall plaque or an old wedding dress, for example—are playthings because they provide some emotional effect, convey a memory, or strike a mood.

All material things are *means* rather than ends in themselves. Tools provide the owner with more free time and leave him with more energy with which to appreciate that free time. Playthings are used to fill the free time and to create an experience of some sort. Playthings are used in an attempt to construct or convey a certain psychological event—a memory, the exhilaration of adventure, the feeling of peace, or contentment. Possessions, then, do not have a value in themselves but are a means to the creation of certain types of experiences.

The characteristic abundance of late capitalist society has created a socio-psychological situation where the possession of things is more or less guaranteed, at least for the middle and upper classes. As a result, modern man need not concentrate on acquiring possessions. Instead, he has become involved and preoccupied with the creation of certain experiences. This, in turn, has become the new focus of the media, of industry, and of modern life.

When man has to struggle for material goods, he is naturally more possessive of them. Holding onto a pair of shoes becomes important when one must make them last a year or go without. But when that same pair is easily gotten and replaced, the shoes themselves lose their significance. The more lucrative a society and the more free-flowing material goods become, the less important any particular article is, and the less emphasis the individual places on ownership as a means of orientation in general. By this process, the cycle of production and consumption pushes the individual to a higher psychological plateau. This does not mean that we will, as a society, produce or consume any less, but merely that we have become less psychologically preoccupied with the ownership of those things that are produced and consumed.

The situation we now find ourselves in is that of a society of inherently acquisitive individuals who no longer *need* to be acquisitive. But our long need-frustrated past is with us still. We are literally exhibiting a "want" hangover. Though the fortunate in our society have all they need, we manufacture more and keep on wanting. Advertising promotes the diversification of these desires, the satisfaction of which funds more advertising for still more products. This is the cycle in which Having man is caught; he is an "addict" of possession in the strictest sense of the word. Even this proliferation of many different types and brands of material goods, however, is insufficient to satisfy the growing number of those who demand a different kind of satisfaction—gratification by experience. Modern man wants to *do,* not to *have.*

This situation has created an interesting paradox. Ours is a society that *wants,* though it need not do so. Further, we have gained more free time, only to find that we do not know how to fill it. What is needed in our times is a new set of goals to "want," a new brand of "goods" to acquire.

The evolution of human consciousness is a series of progressive refinements—in predisposition, in thought, and in action. The shift from Having man, to whom possession is paramount, to Doing man, who holds experience as highest value, is marked by the realization that possession is only a *means* to personal experience. Now, we must make a further refinement. We must understand that collecting random experience is a means to only a particular kind of satisfaction. Increasingly people are looking in new directions to find another experience—a vision of the transcendent. Still others continue to wander ancient avenues seeking a similar goal. The modern popularity of alcohol and drugs is one such direction. A great portion of the modern use of consciousness-altering drugs is not motivated by the hope for desensitization and escape, but rather for stimulation and transcendence.

Alcohol, Drugs, and Modern Man's Traveling Medicine Show

Perhaps the most visible and socially significant form of experience-consumption is drug and alcohol use. (Here the term "drug" will be used to include alcohol.) Recent statistics show an alarmingly high percentage of people in our society who use and/or abuse drugs.

Paradoxically, we have the highest proportion of non-drinkers of any country in the world, except for a few Moslem countries which have outlawed alcohol. (One-third of Americans totally abstain from alcohol.) But we also have the world's worst alcohol problem. The number of those who use narcotics, stimulants, and tranquilizers is very high, as it is for cigarette-smoking. The majority of young adults from age eighteen to twenty-five have tried marijuana, and half of these are regular users, while the use of cocaine is escalating.

Already so much has been written on the causes and effects of drug use, abuse, and addiction, that a comprehensive overview would be futile and presumptuous. Rather, I simply wish to add one dimension to an already complex subject. While many of the causes of drug use have been delineated—including a matrix of biological, psychological, and social factors, combinations of which vary among individuals—one important element has been largely ignored. Drug use must be analyzed not only from the static standpoint of what man is as a complex of causes and factors, but from the vantage point of what he can become. We must investigate the function that drug use plays from a developmental point of view.

In *The Addicted Society* Joel Fort, the nation's leading expert on drug and alcohol use, examines a number of factors contributing to the prevalence of drug use in our culture. Though a variety of factors, biological and psychological, are in operation, Fort concludes that drug use and abuse is largely a *social* disease—the product of a neurotic culture. A number of such factors include peer group pressure, the allure of doing what is forbidden, pleasure-seeking, and social escapism. But Fort barely suggests one other powerful socio-psychological component. Drug abuse may be a misguided attempt to gain self-insight and self-development. Before continuing, however, I will briefly respond to some of these other commonly advanced socio-psychological theories of drug use.

As already mentioned, what has commonly been called

"peer group pressure" is quoted as a major cause of the prevalence of drug use. Doubtless, this is one important factor, but it has been greatly overemphasized. The theory is often self-servingly propounded by parents, teachers, and administrators in an attempt to remove responsibility from a basically "clean" individual onto a rather nebulous environment. However, peer group pressure does not explain why an individual often maintains the habit in the absence of social pressure, nor does it explain why one individual often "turns on" other formerly "clean" individuals. In short, peer group pressure may partially explain why the individual starts using drugs, but not the continuing use in situations without peer pressure.

A second oft-cited factor is the "criminogenic" effect—the mystique of the unknown and the desire to do something illegal. By this view, individuals experiment with drugs from a sense of rebellion, to do what they have been enjoined from, and to taste the forbidden fruit. Once again, there is without doubt a certain amount of truth in this theory. Some historians have argued that the popularity of drinking intoxicating liquor was never as high as during prohibition. Similarly, the use of illicit drugs finds at least some of its impetus in the adventure and intrigue of doing something illegal. But a greater significance has been attributed to this than it deserves. It does not explain the use of alcohol and other legal drugs, nor does it explain continuous use for a period long beyond that which would inspire short-term experimental or rebellious use.

A third story often told is that alcohol and drug use is motivated by the desire to escape from the world, from reality, or from oneself. It is true that a certain amount of drug use is precipitated by the need for relief from anxiety or to "let off steam" (in its milder version) or completely to obviate contact with reality (in its more extreme version). But one must be cautious of the implications of this view. Not only does the motive for use vary from individual to individual, but the effects of various drugs may themselves reveal the underlying purpose for use. For example, use of sedatives may well find its animus in escapism, in dulling the senses and obliterating consciousness. On the other hand, it is unlikely that anyone ever ingested 500 micrograms of LSD in the hope of anxiety release. Desire for novelty or adventure would inspire use of hallucinogenic drugs. Still other substances, notably alcohol, may have diverse effects on different individuals; it obviously provides relaxation for one and stimulation for another, by blocking inhibition.

The language of users provides further insight into the motives for drug use. From "getting high" to the all-engrossing "partying"—hardly a term born of escapism—drug slang evinces images from buoyant hedonism to total transcendence. Current drug use, particularly among the young, is often not the result of tension, frustration, or anxiety, nor the desire to elude today's problems. To the contrary, if there is any wide-scale motivation, it is confrontational. If "escapist" at all, it is not to escape *from* anything so much as it is to escape *to* something greater.

Although admittedly other important motives are operative, we can still ask, what is this search that has fueled the "drug revolution"? It is the pursuit of adventure, of something different; it is an attempt at event legitimatization, born of the desire to resacralize certain times and experiences; it is the desire for a new world, and perhaps a whole new self. In the words of Lifton, the larger meaning of the drug revolution is a result of "seeking a sense of immortality in the way mystics always have, through psychic experience of such great intensity that time and death are, in effect, eliminated." He adds that "renewal on a large scale is impossible to achieve without forays into danger, destruction and negativity" (Lifton 1970, 42-43).

A great deal has been written on the effects of psychedelic drugs and the process of self-development. Numerous writers, thinkers, and philosophers, from Walter Houston Clark to Aldous Huxley, have written of the potential uses and benefits of the use of psychedelic drugs. But even of those who advocate controlled and occasional use of drugs, not one considers it a path unto itself. Rather, the use of drugs may open up new horizons and demonstrate that there are possibilities for psychological functioning completely beyond everyday waking consciousness, thus inspiring interest in traditional forms of self-help. Drugs may facilitate working through psychological blocks, as Roger Walsh suggests in his article "Psychedelics and Self Actualization" (Walsh 1983). All agree, however, that, at best, drug experimentation may stimulate an interest in self-insight and self-development, but it is no substitute for serious self-discipline in the form of meditation, concentration, yoga, or other systems of self-integration. Further, once one of these forms of self-development is begun, any form of drug use—including alcohol—is at best distracting and at worst detrimental (see Chapter 10).

Few drug users today pursue this avocation with the self-conscious determination of some of the writers just mentioned. Nonetheless, the willingness to investigate and experiment with psychoactive substances represents, in many cases, a desire to experience a new mode of psychological functioning. At worst, this may be one phase in the random consumption of experience typical of Doing man. It may—and, in fact, has—inspired some to seek genuine routes of self-transformation. What are these avenues and where do they lead? In the next chapter, I will describe and analyze my own personal experience with meditation.

IV

Metamorphosis: The Enlightened Society

9
A New Image of Humankind: A Personal Account

To this point, this book has been theoretically oriented, with an emphasis on outlining an underlying metaphysical and psychological theory of evolution. If one has had the impression that all this talk of self-transformation was only abstract "stuff and nonsense"—a metaphysic without a reality, a rarefied world view to replace one or another previous paradigm, equally inefficient in winning genuine *moral* and *existential* conviction, I hope now to dispel that suspicion. I consider the last seven years of my life something of an objective, if not "scientific," experiment. I believe, as a result of this experiment, that evolution is a process that may be augmented, encouraged along the lines that await us. We may take a part in our own evolution. Life should be—and can be—a process of always getting better. Everything we do should add up to making each of us more wise, compassionate, humane and, yes, happy as individuals. Life *should* be a process of accumulation, but it is wisdom and love that should be accumulated.

What follows is a very personal, idiosyncratic, and sometimes embarrassing account of my own experience with meditation and the effects it has had on my life. I say "embarassing" because some of the things I am about to relate I would not have readily believed had I read them seven years ago. On the other hand, I should stress that none of the effects are beyond the scope of a naturalistic, as opposed to a supernatural, explanation. The reader may be disappointed to learn that no accounts of ESP, telepathy, telekinesis, or other similar activities will appear. What has transpired is simply an overall physical, emotional, intellectual, and *spiritual* revitalization the likes of which are seldom reported in the annals of modern psychology. As far as I am concerned, this is much more important than psycho-telecommunication, even if such occurrences are a reality.

Before beginning, I should issue three provisos. First, because every person is unique with diverse capacities, interests, and propensities, each develops along different lines and actualizes different abilities. Thus, what occurred in my case cannot be generalized to other individuals. Instead, this account is offered to establish that revitalization in general is possible, though each individual's development will be different.

The second caveat is that diverse forms of meditation have differing effects, as discussed in earlier chapters. For the past seven years I have used a popular meditation technique for twenty-five minutes twice a day. Consequently, I am not in a position to compare and contrast other disciplines. I believe many other disciplines—from Zen to image formation to yoga, or combinations of these—may be equally beneficial, despite the claims of superiority by the dogmatic from one or another particular school. Still, I cannot confirm this from my own experience. I am convinced, however, that the *types* of effects, not the *extent* of transformation, may be diverse. As stated before, different types of meditation, like various types of physical exercise, will enhance different capacities. Further, I think it is important to choose a technique in which one may receive continued instruction, with a teacher readily available to answer questions as the practice develops.

The third and final caveat to what follows is simply that I have had no control group for my "experiment."

Consequently, it is not clear to what degree the changes I am about to describe are the product of meditation, and to what extent they would have occurred with time anyway. Comparing my own experiences with those of others my own age, however, I feel confident that the lion's share of what has transpired is the direct result of meditation.

Initial Effects

When I took up meditation as an experiment, my attitude toward it at that point was a combination of skepticism and cautious hope. I was inspired to begin by a general feeling of dissatisfaction with my life, a feeling that something was missing, and the conviction that somehow it should be possible for me to become a more complete human being. Along with an estimated twenty percent of the American public, I suffered from chronic depression; I also suffered periods of vague melancholia and a disturbing lack of motivation. As a result of this—and perhaps equally a partial cause because bad habits tend to reinforce one another—I drank too much.

Philosophically, I was troubled as well. As a student of modern philosophy, I held a reductionistic materialistic outlook that made it difficult to believe that anything other than a physical modification in brain chemistry could effect a mental change. Thus, I did not think meditation was in spirit consistent with materialism. (Theoretically, it is possible to reconcile materialism with the effects of meditation. Insofar as the act of meditation would be strictly identical to a modification of brain chemistry, a reconciliation is *logically* possible, though for other reasons I reject this approach.) The other general paradigmatic problem I had was a result of the fact that meditation has traditionally been associated with a host of philosophical doctrines thoroughly rejected by modern philosophy. Metaphysical idealism and panpsychism, along with a stifling, otherworldly asceticism, made the prospect of living in accordance with an accompanying life-discipline unthinkable. Luckily, I began my own intellectual reconciliation of Western thought with Eastern discipline and have since found my life to be the happy result of the unlikely marriage of two disparate ideologies.

My first experience with meditation was truly revolutionary. Never before had I so intimately confronted my own psyche. That by simply repeating a thought one could engage oneself so thoroughly left me spellbound. I came to see mental life in terms of an equation of two inversely proportional factors. The more thoughts change, the more the level of consciousness remains fixed. The more a thought itself remains fixed, the more the general level of consciousness changes. If I may be allowed the metaphor, moving from thought to thought in our everyday pattern of thinking is like a stone skipping across the surface of the water. It is only when we think one thought repeatedly —analogous to the stone stopping at one place—that the mind (stone) is able to sink to hitherto unfathomed depths. (I apologize to any who have not yet had this experience for both the use of metaphor and the imprecise manner with which I have written of the distinction between thought, as an act, and consciousness, as a state or context of the thought. I simply believe this is the most illustrative way of describing the initial experience.)

Though the distinction between thought and the context of consciousness seemed appropriate at first, it soon became an illusory distinction. In the first experiences with meditation, I was awed by the way one particular "thought"—one word, image, or other form of mantra—undergoes so many changes at different levels of consciousness. For example, a mantra in the form of a word will initially be "heard" intrapsychically; it will be recognized auditorily. As the process continues, however, one may come to "see" the word; one is aware of the mantra in a visual way. I believe this phenomenon approximates the condition known as synesthesia. Some gifted individuals, notably Isaac Newton, had the synesthetic capacity to "see" musical tones. One tone might appear silver, another black, etc. I routinely encountered the synesthetic effect in the process of meditation.

At first it appears as if one thought goes through a series of continuous changes, being perceived in different ways as the process continues. The process is similar to looking at one object through a series of different lenses, some of which change the appearance of the object with respect to a particular sense, while some change the sensory mode itself. In other words, the thought may undergo a series of visual modifications and then be perceived in a completely different way, e.g., no longer visual but auditory.

From the beginning, the changes occurring *outside* of the periods of meditation were noticeable. Perhaps the first difference I recognized was a marked decrease in the feeling of repetitiveness and boredom in the activities of the day. Prior to this, I had been troubled by the feeling that every day was much the same as any other, and that each activity was marked by a dull banality. One of my first experiences was a sense that each day had a significance of its own. This was not an intellectual feeling but rather a lived experience. Even relatively routine activities were transformed from mundane caricatures of acts of every other day into individual, distinct acts, each deserving attention and respect. Simple things began to take on a new significance and bring a new delight. A walk at twilight became preferable to a night in a crowded bar. An intimate conversation with close friends far surpassed the excitement of hobnobbing with a variety of loose acquaintances. I felt the uniqueness of all things, and a refreshed and revitalized delight in attending to everyday matters became more important. In the term of medieval scholasticism, things and events began to take on a greater level of *haecceitas*—"thisness." All things in the world began to take on an incredible singularity and distinctness. This included both things and events.

The appearance of uniqueness eventually came to affect the meditation itself. Previously there had been one "thought" through different lenses; now there was simply constantly changing thought. What previously had appeared to be a modification in my consciousness of a single thought, I came to understand as different thoughts. Each act of awareness constituted a separate thought. Though each of these might refer to the same external object—one can think about his house, the external object, in a variety of different ways—the thoughts themselves were unique and never stayed the same. I saw that the very essence of the process of thought is *change*.

Another subjective transformation experienced from the beginning was a heightened sensitivity to things. I became more aware of subtle changes in my body. I began to notice certain changes in mood that preceded physical illness by a day or two. These same changes occurred consistently whenever I was about to develop a cold or minor sickness. As a result of this "advance warning," I am able to take precautions to prevent illness.

This increased sensitivity, positive as it was in most cases, could have "negative" effects. For example, it became increasingly difficult to engage in certain activities which were previously easily done. The sound of loud music, the experience of a crowded nightclub, and a number of other sensory stimuli became painful. Cigarette smoke became increasingly unbearable, as did the effects of intoxicating liquor. I found that when I had gone for weeks without a drink, the effects of the meditation seemed to increase, conveying a deepened sensitivity which, in turn, made the effects of even a small amount of wine unpleasant. This was accompanied by a disturbing dullness of mind and a shallower, choppy breathing pattern.

With time I experienced what I can only describe as a heightened sense of awareness. First, my attention span seemed indefinitely lengthened, so that I could sit and work for hours at a time without the need for a break. Also, the *quality* of awareness was enhanced. Not only did I gain a level of motivation I had never known before, but those previously uncontrollable distractions in thought, which effectively sapped a large percentage of the time devoted to work, were eliminated. There were fewer and fewer daydreams and less time wasted on unnecessary mental digressions. I began to awake each morning with a feeling of vibrance and energy rather than apprehension and lethargy, and eagerly involved myself in the day's activities.

This sense of deepened awareness manifested itself in other situations as well. At times, particularly for a few hours after meditation, I experienced an acute alertness, a feeling of undeviating receptivity to external stimuli. This occurred without my attention being led from an external object to internal daydreams, worries, or fantasies. I was *in control* of my mind and could consciously direct its course. Nor was this augmented alertness accompanied by increase in nervous anxiety which characterizes the use of caffeine or other stimulants. Rather, it was a calm alertness, a smooth, free-flowing power of attention devoid of the hypernervous effects.

Within the first few months I began to notice a general lowered anxiety level in a number of areas of my life. At first, I feared that my life was becoming monotone. The emotional lows were less frequent but so, I thought, were the highs. Eventually I realized, however, that many of what I had previously considered "highs" were forms of anxiety release, and these became increasingly unimportant. In their place I felt a delightful equanimity. *All* days were getting better. There was less need for distinguishing "work days" from "play days," good times from bad times, Saturdays from Mondays and, in short, sacred moments from profane hours. What Maslow called the work/joy dichotomy began to dissolve.

It should be noted that all of these effects were gradual and cumulative. There were good days and bad days those first few years, though a definite trend for the better became discernible. There were periods of spiritual drought and of backsliding into old behavior patterns. Though these instances became less frequent, there were times when I thought I was not making any progress whatsoever. Eventually, there would be "breakthroughs"—minor transitions which seemed to mark my progress and open up new levels of experience. In this way, the slow progression of development was perpetuated.

The Experience of Meditation

As mentioned, my periods of meditation, performed for twenty-five minutes twice a day, were typically accompanied by a series of progressions in my perception of the mantra. It could be visual or auditory, though I never experienced it in a tactile mode, nor have I ever "smelled" or "tasted" the mantra. After a while I began to experience the mantra less in a sensory manner and more cognitively. This experience might be similar to the way we cognize abstract concepts such as peace, war, or justice. I did not think of the *sound* of the word or some visual icon or symbol; rather it became increasingly abstract. This was sometimes confusing. Often the experience would be analogous to attempting to think of a word that one cannot remember. In one sense we "know" the word. We may be able to state what it means or give examples of it, and there is some unconscious object toward which we are directing our memory. Yet we cannot *name* the word itself. Similarly, there were (and are) often times when the mantra was not represented in awareness in a conceptual or sensory mode, and yet I was somehow "thinking" it.

Occasionally after events like this I had a powerful experience—the object of all meditation—the experience of pure awareness, consciousness without an object. These moments were fleeting, and description is difficult. Basically, the event is marked by an awareness that is not sensory or cognitive. It is as if I had been stripped of contact with both the outer and inner worlds, isolated from all intrapsychic representation of anything objective.

When this occurs, one does not "see black" because this would be a sensory manifestation. One is not aware of silence, for even this is to think about something. The mantra has completely disappeared, and there is not even awareness that there is no object of awareness, for this also would be a "thought." There is simply awareness devoid of all objects, a condition as psychologically powerful as it is intellectually perplexing. Generally, the first thought to succeed this all-too-brief experience is, "This is pure awareness!" The occurrence of even this thought, of course, is a signal that the experience has come to an end.

The aftermath of the experience of pure awareness is marked by a feeling of deep emotional release. There is a profound equanimity that overtakes the mind, and a feeling of joy that is greatly rewarding. The experience will then color the hours and days afterward with a tranquility and feeling of grace.

The description of these transcendent experiences leads me to a peripheral issue. I should say here that I dislike the connotations of the word "mystic" and I do not consider myself a mystic in the sense in which the word is usually used. First, I do not embrace the popular conception of the mystical world view. I do not believe evil is illusory; to the contrary I believe it is often more "real" than the good in this world. Further, I am not resigned to the world, but am committed to changing it. I do not know what it means to say that all plurality is illusion. I suspect that most of those who hold such a view do not know what it means either. (Those who have attempted to explain it to me talk as if they believe there is a *physical* unity among all things, a view that is obviously wrong because one physical thing can be changed or destroyed without modifying another thing. Further, if we are told that everything "is one" in that all share the property of "Being," then I must accept this. Yes, all things that exist share one quality in common—they all exist—but this sounds viciously circular to me.)

A great deal of pseudo-philosophy has recently

accompanied the popularization of mysticism and the occult. This is unfortunate, I believe, because it only serves to give a bad name to what I take to be a fundamental set of experiences—experiences that I myself have had. Meditation and other forms of psycho-spiritual self-discipline must be extricated from the popular paradigm with which they are affiliated and cast in a new light, the light of science and worldly humanism.

During the experience of meditation, a variety of other perceptions and occurrences may temporarily grab one's attention. For example, I encountered a series of distortions in the way I experienced my body. I felt that it was elongating, flowing into an abnormally long, sinuous form. Sometimes, my head would tingle while an amazing display of light filled the inner sky. Often, I would feel like a disembodied mind, losing perception of the rest of my body until, just to be certain, I would wiggle a finger or shift a leg. Ultimately, all such occurrences were pleasant distractions from which I gently withdrew to the inner sanctum of the mantra.

Another set of phenomena worthy of note is what I believe to have been the re-experiencing of old stresses. Stories abound of people briefly feeling assorted pains or discomforts, later to find that as children they had been hurt in the area where the feeling had occurred. In my own case, I often resurrected memories of things I had not recalled in years, re-experienced these events, and then moved on. There was also a most interesting period near the beginning of my work with meditation when I would emerge from the sessions feeling quite intoxicated. It wasn't a completely subjective state either; on a number of occasions friends remarked that I looked and moved like an intoxicated person. This occurred occasionally for a few months, lasting no more than an hour after meditation. The only explanation I can muster is that, in purifying oneself, some of the old stresses briefly re-appear.

Finally, the body responds to meditation in an interesting and physiologically significant way. With absorption comes a slowing of the metabolism. The heartbeat decreases, and the breathing becomes so subdued at times that one would appear not to be breathing at all. An entire range of tests have been conducted to measure these and other responses, including EEG, blood pressure, and the galvanic skin response, described in many books on meditation.

A Springtime Transition

After about two years of faithful practice, it seemed I had gotten into a rut. Events in life can have a profound effect on meditation, just as meditation can affect one's life. The negative consequence of this reciprocal relationship is that when life is not moving along so smoothly, an otherwise somewhat "dry" period of meditation can become almost unbearable. In my case uncertainty as to my ultimate direction in life, accompanied by waning employment prospects, contributed to an unfortunate psychological situation. Though I had largely overcome my long, intermittent bouts with depression, the old condition came roaring back with a vengeance seldom experienced before. I began to drink more frequently, though much less than two years earlier, and other external conditions were far from optimal. The meditation periods became trials of endurance; I seemed to derive absolutely no positive benefits from them.

When it seemed I had reached the bottom, both inwardly and in other areas of my life, I came very near to quitting everything, renouncing the experiment as the search for a will-o'-the-wisp. It was when I had reached this emotional nadir that I developed the urge to do some reading from esoteric literature. I then resolved to isolate myself for a week, to spend the time reading, fasting, and meditating six times a day. I decided that if things did not change by the end of the week, I would cut my losses, discontinue meditating, and resume the search for a better way. I now believe this week was the turning point in my life.

During this week-long fast, the intensity of the meditation did not seem to change or deepen, and yet as the week progressed there developed a different quality—an experience of profound restfulness. By the time I broke the fast on Friday night of that unforgettable week, a new feeling of vigor and optimism seemingly coursed through my nervous system. I had no mystical interludes to report, no transcending the subject/object dichotomy, nothing that in the least smacked of the supernatural. And yet I was revitalized. I had won a new self. And the best was yet to occur.

In the weeks that followed, I began gradually but systematically to change numerous aspects of my life. Some of the changes were conscious and deliberate, while others just seemed to happen to fill out the parameters of a renewed existence. Many were simple things. I began awaking earlier. I accomplished more during each day. I began exercising regularly. More importantly, new ideas revealed themselves to me each day. I was more alive, more creative, and at the same time, I achieved greater equanimity of mind.

In the weeks immediately after the transitional week, my meditation regularly reached a depth I had seldom experienced before. I measure "depth" in terms of three factors—the intensity of the psychological experience; the degree of quieting the physiological responses (breath and heart rate); and effects outside of the meditation. In all three dimensions the results were well beyond even the best days at an earlier stage of development.

Perhaps the greatest external impact this period had on my life was a completely gradual, natural, and non-deliberate conversion to vegetarianism. Previous to this, I did not have the least inclination toward such a diet. I enjoyed meat and had never entertained the slightest interest in what I would have considered such an exotic diet. But gradually I became less interested in eating meat. It was not an aversion or positive disgust with the carnivorous or omnivorous diet that brought about my "conversion," and even today I am not particularly averse to the taste of meat. Rather, I simply became less interested in eating meat, and one day decided simply to refrain altogether. As strange as it sounds, this was the easiest thing I have ever done. No will power or conscious deliberation was required. I have, in a manner resembling operant self-conditioning, found that a properly balanced vegetarian diet facilitates improved concentration, greater energy, and a healthier state of mind and body. I do not claim that this diet would work similarly for everyone, but in my own case I have found vegetarianism to be a vast improvement over an alternative diet.

Perhaps the most significant effect that I attribute to the vegetarian diet is that of eliminating, once and for all, that gnawing melancholia and depression that even meditation alone did not previously ameliorate. Since modifying my diet—I still eat eggs, milk, and other dairy products—I have not experienced one period of depression. Of course, I am still capable of sadness, grief, and the entire range of negative emotions. The difference is that now when they occur they are triggered by *external* events, not by a capricious and destructive internal chemistry. When I experience sadness, it is a predictable response to external contingencies; it is not a mood. Further, I have more control over these emotions when they do occur. Perhaps just as significantly, no longer am I victimized by the debilitating lack of motivation that marked the earlier periods of depression. On a few occasions this lack of drive was so complete that I could not muster the will even to walk across the room. Now I believe I have cured myself, and I have done so without the need for stimulants or other drugs commonly administered to the seriously depressed. I hope that what I have written here does not have the tone of a confession or the pretentiousness of a "Ten Days to a New You" best-seller. Mine has been a successful search and a struggle to win optimum mental health.

With respect to vegetarianism, I believe there are psysio-chemical reasons for the effects of certain foods on mental health. These effects have not been seriously studied by science. Whether it is the additives or preservatives used to process meat, the chemicals used in stimulating growth while the animal is still alive, or simply the chemicals released just prior to death which bring about the negative mental effects, it is clear to me that these effects are real. (Some hold that the way in which some animals are slaughtered may cause the release of a large quantity of adrenaline and other neurochemicals in the epinephrine family, a result of the "fight or flight" response. These chemicals remain in the meat after death and may have an adverse effect on those who consume it.)

In order further to verify my belief that the vegetarian diet is beneficial, I performed yet one more set of experiments on myself. Maintaining all other habits and routines, I gradually reintroduced poultry and seafood into my diet. Within a few days the effect was noticeable and unmistakable. A different state of mind developed—heavier, more morose, and more compulsive. Meditation lost its depth and intensity. I felt the entire experiment had returned me to that previous state of mind from which I had hoped to escape. There were also some physical changes: notably, a stiffening of the muscles and joints, accompanied by a loss of flexibility and vigor. I repeated this same experiment a year later with similar results.

I must confess that I am not certain what to make of the results of these "experiments." I surely did not start with the intention of becoming an advocate of the vegetarian diet. However, the change in diet has helped me a great deal and I simply wish to report these results. A similar change may or may not work for others, but the results are reported with the hope that others will "replicate" them and find them helpful. I do believe that, if science one day finds biochemical reasons for what I have described, we will be confirming what many in faraway cultures have known and lived by for centuries. Experience often precedes empirical verification, and what is believed to work for one reason may in reality work for quite another. For example, the American Indians believed that their sacrifice of small fish buried near each plant would secure the survival of the plant. Modern science tells us that this indeed did work, though the reason is that the decomposition of the fish enriched the soil with nitrogen. Similarly, ancient ways of life cultivated by the Oriental cultures may also have the effects that have long been attributed to them. In this view vegetarianism is not so much a moral discipline as it is a healthy way of living. Its effects—enhanced mental control—are the natural results of a corresponding way of life.

This same principle of ancient experience and modern verification may have broader implications as well. Traditional practices such as meditation, yoga, maintaining equanimity of mind, and vegetarianism may all have the very results that have been traditionally attributed to them. It is up to modern science, however, to explain why. Furthermore, it is up to modern philosophy and, on a larger scale, the humanities to construct a new paradigm, a new image of man, which combines this ancient experiential knowledge with our modern social and scientific understanding. Specifically, we must extricate psycho-spiritual discipline and its surrounding behavior patterns, from the pessimistic, ascetic and otherworldly connotations with which they are commonly associated. Only then will larger numbers of people feel free to experiment and incorporate such patterns into their own lives.

My "experiment" is now nearly seven years old. What started out as a sort of mental exercise has become an integral part of my life. While my original goal was physical and psychological health, I now feel the rewards of this way of life are beginning to extend beyond these levels, at least as they are traditionally viewed. Yoga and meditation, practiced the first thing each morning and again before dinner, have brought a deepened self-direction to a moral and spiritual level. I begin each meditation period with a thought of how, in one way or another, I must improve as a person. Then I devote that period to that particular goal, concentrating on one or two such goals over a period of months. I call this activity "spiritual" in deference to traditional systems of philosophy which separate the "psychological" (the rational and emotional capacities) from those that were supposed to be functions of the soul (moral development, the ability to love, or the propensity for self-insight).

In the end, self-development is a gradual process, though discrete. Development seems to come in stages, bursts of growth followed by periods of slow progression or plateaus. But, whatever else it is, self-development through meditation should not be the subject of fads or on-again off-again experimentation. It should be a lifelong commitment, just as existence itself must be a lifelong commitment to oneself to always seek to improve, to get better as a person. Self-realization is not the process of moving beyond humanity. Quite to the contrary, it is humanity that is the goal of enlightenment.

A Note on Spiritual Imperialism and Consumerism

I wish to close this chapter with a few words on my experience as an observer of the "spiritual marketplace." What I say may well be applicable to most modern schools, disciplines, or movements. Since I think it is unfortunate that any spiritual force should be politicized, and I believe that spiritual growth is a singularly personal thing, I disdain the use of the term "movement" in this context. Still, I must acknowledge that some sort of network for the dissemination of this knowledge is essential.

I will set forth the following, a result of my own experience, as rules or principles in imperative form. I do not do this for an authoritative effect, or to set myself apart as an expert. I am not. Rather, these are my own conclusions which I believe will be helpful to those troubled by similar concerns.

First, never believe anyone who claims that his form of meditation or system of self-discipline is better than all others. This claim is made by a number of currently popular schools, including the one in which I learned to meditate. Some techniques will be better than others for some people. But no one can claim that one technique is superior to all others for all people. Those who make this claim generally have not used any system other than the one they are touting. They are simply repeating what others, equally as inexperienced, have told them. Even those who have tried a few other systems before settling into the now-favored discipline cannot make the determination of superiority for all others. Finally, and significantly, chances are that the claims of superiority are motivated by either spiritual insecurity, the need to proselytize to reconfirm one's own faith, or an insipid economic motive. In any case, such claims are as poorly motivated as they are grossly unfounded.

My advice to the seeker is to ignore the claims, but to make a definite commitment to a system for a predetermined period of time. There is the advantage to a systemized technique that the same method has been tried by others and you will know what you are getting, and that it has been used successfully by others. If you are unhappy with the results, move on. However, all of these systems take years to have their deepest effects. One should therefore be fully educated as to all of the available options before commitment to one system or another.

Second, be concerned with the technique or the system for self-improvement, not with the leader of the movement. Spiritual revitalization degenerates into idol worship when a charismatic personality becomes the focus. In fact, this is the most important characteristic of a cult. Too frequently I have seen the "student" become the "follower" with universally pernicious effects. Time should be spent in self-assessment instead of being squandered telling stories about the guru or recounting his latest movements. I find this personally distressing. There is a fine line between instruction and worship; I fear that line is crossed too frequently.

Third, incorporating the method of self-development into one's life does not mean adopting the entire underlying philosophy and metaphysics. I have heard some of the most outrageous, naive, and self-contradictory claims at group meditation meetings, often made by teachers. With pontifical authority, I have heard teachers discoursing on such varied subjects as the nature of ultimate reality, the existence of God, the essence of knowledge, and a plethora of other similar topics. Often, these teachers have little or no philosophical training. Many of their claims are as contrary to common sense as they are philosophically amusing. In my own case, I was lucky enough to have a teacher who was as philosophically astute as he was honest. He never made incredible claims and kept the learning process "scientific."

The lesson to be learned is that the student should feel comfortable with dissociating the technique in which he is interested from the underlying philosophy propounded by the school or movement. A school that does not permit one to retain his traditional religious or philosophical outlook should be avoided; it may be a downright dangerous influence.

One of the largest complaints directed at some organizations is that there is something profoundly "unspiritual" about selling meditation. I am ambivalent about this issue. The movements offer a host of reasons for the price they charge. A common one is the necessity to compensate the teacher for his time, which I believe is legitimate. However, the curious rationale that the average consumer will not take the process as seriously if he does not pay for it, that investment acts as an added incentive to practice faithfully, is at best questionable. It seems as disingenuous as it appears derogatory of the technique. If meditation is so powerful and effective, what need is there for external incentives to encourage its practice?

I cannot render a blanket statement for all systems, or all prices. My own investment, though it seemed high at the time, was probably the most worthwhile expenditure of my life. I am certain I have been compensated a thousandfold for the cost of learning to meditate. Thus, I would recommend that if a person has carefully researched a system, thinks he will be happy with it, and can without pang of conscience afford it, he should make the investment.

There is a great deal more that needs to be said on the issue of the selling of meditation, as well as about the methods used to interest prospective students in various schools. Often, on becoming familiar with the situation, one is convinced that there is something deeply unsavory about the way in which both have occurred. Disingenuous selling pitches and self-proclaimed gurus abound and have served to provide us with the twentieth-century analogue of P.T. Barnum's comment that a sucker is born every minute. I write in the hope that I might convince those seeking a way to better themselves to maintain both vigilance and an open mind. Genuine possibilities do exist. This chapter has been written to present my own experience in this matter.

Meditation is an on-going process. In spite of my many imperfections, the process has changed me for the better in a number of respects. And it continues to do so. Whether anything approximating true enlightenment will be my lot in life will have to wait for my last book, rather than my first. At this point, however, the prospect appears undeniably within the realm of possibility.

10
The True Goal of Religion

When Albert Einstein first came to the United States, it is reported that he was asked by a judge, as part of his test for citizenship, whether he believed in God. Einstein, not believing in the personal God of the Christian faith, is reported to have answered, "God? Why, yes. I believe in the God of Spinoza." The philosophically naive judge accepted this, not realizing that Spinoza's God was none other than nature, the laws of science, and all that exists in the world.

Some of the greatest personages in history, such as Socrates, Spinoza, and Einstein, while not "pious" in any traditional sense and often questioning or outright rejecting the religion of their day, nonetheless lived genuinely "spiritual" lives. Spinoza's compassion and selfless bravery as he turned the riotous mob away from his house when it came to lynch his beloved companion, Socrates' joyful equanimity in the face of death, and Einstein's many humanitarian campaigns serve as examples of a deeper sense of duty. Even the half-mad Nietzsche, while advocating the unconditional abrogation of Christian faith and doctrine and sham morality, exhibited at many times a spiritual orientation to life. In a pathetic and ironic episode near the end of his life when he had become completely insane from syphilis, he came upon a man brutally whipping a horse. Nietzsche pummeled the man and then fell upon the horse, sobbing violently as he hugged the bewildered animal in the middle of traffic. Through history, there have been many such incidents, some more peculiar than others, performed by spiritual persons who are not necessarily "religious."

It has become all too clear in the work done in the psychology of religion to date that no single set of criteria will serve as necessary and sufficient conditions for what is deemed "religious." Even such traditional doctrinal mainstays as belief in a supernatural deity or a personal afterlife have been rejected in the light of certain findings that some religions have not integrated such beliefs into their superstructures. As Walter Houston Clark has noted, religion is different things to different people.

> The psychologist of religion faces some formidable problems. Even the definition of religion is a matter of great dispute. Several years ago I asked a number of experts in the field of the scientific study of religion to define what they meant by the word *religion*. Of 68 replies no two were exactly alike, and even when replies were grouped the categories differed. This is hardly a happy situation to any discipline making any pretense to being a science (Clark 1977, 230).

Perhaps the term "religious," like most other words in our language, has no clear boundaries or specific criteria for application. As with the word "game," it connotes a large group of roughly similar practices and beliefs that have only a general family resemblance. There are no specific characteristics that delineate the term "religious" in all religious practices, and likewise, no set of general characteristics can be found that are sufficient to designate any practice under the general rubric. Even jogging, it has been noted, can be practiced in a religious manner, with a devotion and a feeling of ultimacy, and with physical and psychological effects not unlike those reported by the most fervent religious converts.

Insofar as refusal to become embroiled in the disputes

over terminology constitutes a virtue, I will avoid any discussion of limiting parameters of the religious. Instead, acknowledging the ambiguity, I will turn to more specific questions.

The quest for true spirituality far transcends the relatively superficial religious dogma and ritual that accompany various traditional religions. I maintain that the spiritual imperative may at times manifest itself in the various religions of the world, but that the psycho-spiritual drive is itself a quest for something deeper. This search or drive may manifest itself in an infinite plethora of emotional, cognitive, behavioral, and cultural responses. Such responses are shaped by the dictates of a particular society and by the needs of the individual. As psychologist Gordon Allport has written:

> Most psychologists who have written on religion seem agreed that there is no single and unique religious emotion, but rather a widely divergent set of experiences that may be focused upon a religious object. It is the habitual and intentional focusing of experience rather than the character of the experience itself that marks the existence of a religious sentiment (Allport 1950, 4).

No attempt will be made here to reduce all religious experience to a single common denominator. This seems to have been the mistake of many anthropologists, psychologists, and philosophers, and Allport is right in correcting the tendency (Allport 1950, 3-6). A number of reasons will be outlined to explain why religious expression may take many forms. However, I maintain that the religious imperative is a real need, though it may be a very amorphous one, and that this need, like all needs, has arisen to serve an evolutionary function.

The Psycho-Spiritual Need

In Chapter Three it was established that the concept of need is not correctly limited to that of deficit needs.

Higher imperatives as well are needs in the most significant sense of the word. The "psycho-spiritual need" is the term I have applied to that drive, manifest in an infinite number of ways, that seeks to reconcile man with himself, with the cosmos, and with the most sacred and meaningful aspects of what it means to be alive. This urge may manifest itself in devotion to a paternalistic God, in the search for absolute transcendental unity, or in the quest for an innermost self. Whatever the perceived object of the need, that such a need exists is a fundamental assertion.

The Dimensions of Need

At this time it becomes necessary to delve deeper into the nature of the concept of need. There are, by analysis, three aspects of needs: the psychophysiological, the behavioral-expressive, and the teleological or goal directed. These three dimensions are all observable on the level of the psycho-spiritual need.

The psychophysiological component is the physical-chemical, biological, or hormonal aspect of a need along with its subjectively perceived presence: the conscious yearning and passive recognition of a need, along with the underlying physiological patterns that accompany that feeling. It is the raw feeling of hunger, of fatigue, or the desire for affection. It is experienced as amorphous and nondescript, and yet is a mercilessly driving force in the psyche of the individual. It spurs on the search for gratification.

In essence, the behavioral-expressive component of need is the set of behaviors that an organism performs to satisfy a need. This includes not only the objective routine and ritual of the process of satisfaction, but also, at least in man, an internal cognitive aspect. Thus, needs may take on a meaning beyond what is felt and become invested with a cognitive content. For example, sexual arousal is experienced not only as an amorphous visceral feeling, but is accompanied by cognitive images suggesting objects of satisfaction, e.g., an attractive partner. Both the cognitive and behavioral aspects of this component of need may be culturally conditioned.

Unlike the lower needs that are experienced in only one way (e.g., hunger always feels the same), this subjective aspect of the psycho-spiritual need is manifest in a number of ways. The desire for union with the transcendent, for liberation, or for otherworldly guidance are just a few examples of how this need is subjectively realized. It may eventuate in prayer, a devotional service, meditation, or confession, depending on the culture. The individual may further relate to this need by one of a variety of cognitive contents, e.g., a personal God or a departed ancestor. Thus, widely different behaviors and cognitive symbols may be expressions of similar needs. That one person seeks an impersonal Unity while another desires communion with a personal God does not gainsay the possibility that both expressions are reactions to one and the same need.

However, not all behaviors resulting from the subjective recognition of a need are equally effective in satisfying the goal. Certain activities may be more fulfilling than others. For example, an individual who recognizes his own need for love may attempt to satisfy it in a variety of ways. He may find one permanent partner with whom to develop an intimate relationship, or he may take to nightlife, meeting a variety of partners and engaging in a series of different relationships. It may turn out that the first response is more effective than the second in satisfying the need for love. Similarly, the psycho-spiritual need may result in a number of behavioral responses, some of which are more satisfying than others. Ultimately, the effectiveness of a response will be a function of how successfully it fulfills the need.

Needs have evolutionary import. Hunger has an obvious physiological end. But sometimes the actual goal of a need and what we subjectively perceive (as part of the cognitive content) to be the reason for a need may be two different things. An example is the primitive culture that sees sexual intercourse as a means of binding the souls of man and wife, while not realizing the results of the procreative aspect. Evolution is best suited not only by our recognition of various needs, but in the correct perception of the end or goal of that need. Thus, some practices and beliefs are clearly superior to others.

The Laws of Need

Psychologist A.G. Skard has delineated nine laws of organic needs and desires:

1) A need not satisfied tends to store its energy. In short, the first law holds that the denial of a need tends to *increase* its energy. [There are interesting metaphysical implications to the notion of a need "having energy" in a positive sense as opposed to being a deficit of one form or another. What does it mean for a need to "store"—as if it were a container—a certain amount of energy? Unfortunately, there is space only to mention this enigma.]

2) The stronger a need is, the less particular we are about the way we satisfy it. Thus, for example, intense hunger tends to break down previous cultural and individual prohibitions and dislikes, as in the event of eating what would normally be considered distasteful (e.g., cannibalism).

3) Indifference results from excessive indulgence.

4) Social influence may serve to stimulate or inhibit our needs. In the case of the more basic needs, cultural influence tends to direct the need to specific channels, such as the eating of certain foods, rather than actually curbing hunger. (Even outright curbing of needs occurs at times, as in the dieters' craze.)

5) If a strong need remains unsatisfied, other needs tend to be neglected. Lack of sleep often affects the appetite.

6) Needs that are not satisfied may sometimes be replaced by other needs. The reformed alcoholic may take

up coffee and cigarettes, or the faithful husband away from home overeats rather than breaking his vows.

7) Needs often conflict with one another.

8) Needs sometimes combine, rather than conflict, such that one behavior may satisfy a number of needs at once. Eating out serves the dual function of satisfying hunger and the social imperative, as eating is often done in groups.

9) No need can be fulfilled in social isolation. (Oates 1957, 103-105)

I wish to add another law to this list, one which is of great importance:

10) There is a "threshold" of need whereby greater than average indulgence tends to increase the amount of activity required to satisfy the need. Thus, the person who eats a great deal tends to become hungry easily. Curbing his intake may reduce his appetite.

These ten generalizations, nine by Skard and one developed here, are not to be taken as absolute nomic regularities. There are a certain vagueness and an ambiguity and at points even contradictions, as in the seventh and eighth laws. Rather than strict regularities, then, they should be taken as general guidelines and as heuristic devices in discussing the nature of need, and in particular the psychological level of need.

These laws are relevant to the spiritual quest because the nature of the religious imperative, whatever else it may be, is in a very real sense a *need*. Many theories have been elaborated on its origin and ultimate nature. But few if any would argue against the claim that that which calls man to religion is in some sense a *need*, whether the object of its satisfaction is seen as illusory as with Freud, or real as with Tillich, C. S. Lewis, or the Ulanovs, (Ulanov 1975, 39). Insofar as the yearning or desire for meaning, self-transcendence, or communion with God is felt, it is real.

Two questions naturally arise at this time. First, in what way are these various amorphous yearnings—religious, psychological, existential-philosophical—related?

What makes them aspects of the same general need? Second, what is the end or goal of this need? It is in hope of answering these questions that I return to the analysis of the concept of need.

Notice first that the psycho-spiritual need conforms to the tripartite analysis of need in general. First, there is the subjective or felt aspect so often described in religious literature, the intense desire or longing in the heart. This has psychophysiological dimensions, which include certain psychological and even physiological responses. It has been demonstrated, for example, that the strong conviction so endemic of the religious has an effect on the adrenal system, causing the release of endomorphines (Snyder 1975, 90). This may explain the healing effect of certain religious rituals and practices.

Second, as noted, there is a wide variety of behavioral responses with respect to the psycho-spiritual need. Not only is there a seemingly endless plethora of religious belief systems and practices, but each has its own projected end, be it salvation, nirvana, or other.

The third aspect of need is the actual goal of the need, independent of what we may think it is. It is the contention of this book that the psycho-spiritual imperative, like any other human need, can be explained only naturalistically. It has its origin in man, and its end is not that of divine worship or devotion to the Other, but the development of the self and the furtherance of evolution. I maintain that the religious calling—immersed in so many different doctrines, dogmas, and ultimate heresies throughout history and all over the globe—is at bottom none other than the need for an evolution of consciousness in man.

The religious or the psycho-spiritual need can be assimilated to the general concept of need and to the analysis of any physical need. It is growth-oriented and is responsible, in more advanced cases, for a wide variety of styles of individual spiritual development, some of which have been characterized by the term "transpersonal" or beyond the usual bounds of ego-consciousness.

But before continuing with an analysis of such spiritually progressive (and statistically infrequent) cases, let us view the situation of ordinary twentieth-century man. For, if my contention is correct, modern man does not realize that the religious imperative is indeed a real need, the neglect of which must spell ill-health and perhaps the majority of social problems. Nor does he realize that the true satisfaction of this need can be bought only at the price of self-scrutiny, discipline, and a working knowledge of higher states of consciousness. In short, if my contention is accurate, twentieth-century man is analogous to the hungry beast that has not yet learned to eat and manifests a great need that he does not yet know how to satisfy fully.

What I have called the psycho-spiritual need is, from one angle, a nebulous web of related desires. Somehow the quest for individual philosophical or existential meaning gets bound up in the traditionally broader religious question. Further, it is common knowledge that a great deal of psychotic behavior is invested with religious imagery and significance by the patient. There are also numerous studies that demonstrate the existence of a positive relationship between recovery from alcoholism or drug addiction and religious conversion. Religion thus serves as a psychophysiological surrogate for a formerly debilitating habit. Conversely, many a person who has lost the sense of ultimate meaning provided by the religious experience often turns to alcohol or drug abuse. Equally as significant, numerous studies have demonstrated the relationship between existential insecurity or manifest anxiety and sudden religious conversion (Spellman, Baskett, and Byrne 1977, 249-253).

The psycho-spiritual imperative includes many kinds of factors: psychophysiological, as in the case of anxiety; existential, as in the case of personal life tragedies; psychological, as in the case of integrative flaws in the personality structure; and sociopsychological, as in the case of problems related to crime, drug abuse, racism, and alienation. Why? The answer is simple if we refer to the laws of need. The first law holds that unsatisfied needs have a tendency to store and increase their energy. The second holds that unfulfilled needs may be sublimated into other channels and expressed through a variety of different behavior. Thus, indulgence in a variety of mind-altering substances, most often destructive, has the effect of temporarily satisfying the need, though ultimately the true end goes unachieved. Further, the psychological deficit that goes uncompensated may produce a great number of ill effects. The lack of fulfillment may manifest itself inwardly, producing negative psychological and physiological effects and ultimately poor health. Or it may be directed outward in a variety of socially destructive ways.

The fourth law holds that social influence may have stimulating or inhibiting effects on need, and it may also condition the modes of expression. Different cultures will result in different behaviors, some closer to meeting the requisite goal of the need than others. Western culture has placed an emphasis on the lower needs such as for food to such an extent that we now have carefully delineated and highly complex nutritional categories: protein, carbohydrates, vitamins, etc. On the other hand, we have been largely unsuccessful in understanding or satisfying the psycho-spiritual needs. In the East, the converse is true.

There seems to be, at some fundamental level, an underlying connectedness among the needs, as is demonstrated in the fifth law. When certain needs are neglected, others remain unsatisfied as well. Our culture, aside from the obvious failure to countenance the psycho-spiritual need, has had a long history of social alienation. The lack of love, the prevalence of loneliness, the barely veiled presence of hatred for other factions, along with political-economic manipulation and social one-up-manship, are only too obvious from within and without. Thus, large segments of the psychological spectrum of needs remain unsatisfied in the West.

The sixth law holds that needs that are not satisfied are

often replaced by altogether different needs. (This is related to the second law and is a very significant point.) Neglect of higher needs accounts for indulgence in a plethora of destructive behaviors at the individual and cultural levels. Alcoholism, drug-abuse, gratuitous self-aggrandizement, and even the militaristic imperative which led to the death of over a hundred million people in this century alone (Laing 1967, 77-100) have been the vengeful progeny of this neglect.

The ninth law holds that human needs can be satisfied only in the context of social interaction. This is prescriptive as well as descriptive with respect to the current world dilemma. Put simply, teachers and visionaries are needed to guide the young searchers. Scientific research is needed to provide the most efficient means by which the psycho-spiritual needs may be satisfied. Cooperation on a hemispheric scale would bring together the ways of East and West, so that twenty-first century society might become the most synthetic and all-embracing union of the material and the psychological in history. Neither realm should be purchased at the price of the other.

Finally, the tenth law holds that the regular practice of a certain level of activity, done with the intention of need-satisfaction, tends to increase the individual's lust, as well as the quantity of experience needed to satisfy the need. This tendency is most obvious in the psycho-spiritual need when beginning effective spiritual practice creates greater need for the activity, sometimes to the point where the individual rearranges his life accordingly. Conversely, to the novice even a small amount of work or practice can have profound effects upon the nascent individual consciousness.

These ten laws of need lend great explanatory power to the contention that the religious drive cannot be reduced to any one typical form of expression, nor one single psychophysiological origin. The religious impulse may be activated by fear in some, by love in others, and by theoretical awe in a third group, while some seek security and others strive for understanding. For some, religious conversion seems to precipitate mental breakdown, though it is the ultimate integrating force for others. This variation indicates that the network and connections of needs described in the ten laws are active. For some, the sacred may occur in the context of love because the emotional need for love may compensate for, or be exacted in exchange for, the unfulfilled psycho-spiritual need. Fear, anxiety, unity, self-transcendence, and other emotions and aspirations may be intertwined with the religious because of the state of imbalance or dissatisfaction at these levels, including psycho-spiritually. What is important is that the form of behavioral expression and the subjective cognitive content—what the individual perceives to be the object of the need—do not necessarily correlate with the actual goal of the need.

Psycho-Spiritual Need and the Having, Doing, and Being Levels

What is the evolutionary reason, if indeed "reason" is the correct word, that the psycho-spiritual need has emerged? What function does it play in the development of the human race? In other words, what is the true goal of religion?

At the level of Having man, religion is an esoteric means to a material end. Walter Houston Clark has estimated that as many as ninety percent of those who claim to be religious, are *extrinsically* oriented. This means that the individual uses the religious service as a means of social bonding, a way to remain within the fold, not for religious experience but for social expedience. The extrinsically oriented do not live by the principles of the religion. For example, there is a high correlation between such individuals in various Christian denominations and the prevalence of racism and authoritarianism. (The small minority who are *intrinsically* oriented take religious doctrine to heart.) There is a definite correlation between those extrinsically oriented to religion and the Having personality. Havers use religion as a social, political, and economic tool for furthering their own ends.

Religion at the Doing level is the result of an attempt to help restructure the personality, to define one's identity, and to "keep sane." This is a noble goal insofar as personal psychological stability and integrity are necessary conditions to still further growth, but it is preliminary to a greater level of orientation.

It is only at the level of Being that the psycho-spiritual need can be fully attended to. At this point religion ceases to be a social phenomenon, in the usual sense, and instead becomes intensely personal. Here the true goal of religion becomes immanent. The personality becomes oriented to a central core of experiences cultivated by the individual—personal encounters with pure consciousness (see Chapter Two). These have a very significant effect on the personality. In some these experiences are accompanied by sudden and tumultuous, though temporary, shifts in perception, resulting in mystical experiences, experiences of unity, and self-transcendence. Others experience only a gradual refinement of behavior, perhaps accompanied by dietary changes or with improved subjective feelings about the world. Both groups tend to have a gradual shift in moral predisposition, an expansion of intellectual capacity, and general amelioration of psychological and emotional functioning.

The true goal of religion is comprehensive self-development effective at every level of human functioning. One gradually comes to understand oneself better, to realize hidden motivation in the most routine behavior and emotional dispositions, and to communicate more effectively and cooperate better with others. Neurosis is the antithesis of psycho-spiritual progression, a progression that can be measured physically, psychologically, and socially.

On the physical level, psycho-spiritual development is accompanied by overall improvement of one's health. There is little doubt today of the impact good mental health may have on the body. Numerous studies have clearly demonstrated the relationship between psychological stress and physical illness, and the elimination of such stress, resulting from psychological improvement, will effect better overall health. Frequency of colds, susceptibility to minor infectious diseases, and even the probability of developing various forms of cancer and heart disease are greatly reduced (Maslow 1962, 23). Nervous quirks and other minor physical maladies may also be reduced or completely eliminated.

It is on the psychological level, however, that psycho-spiritual growth has its greatest impact. From the gradual overcoming of depression, anxiety, and neurosis to the enhanced sense of self-worth, existential significance, and general levels of motivation and productivity, the signs of growth can be monitored. As this progression continues, the self gains stability and the subject has more energy to invest in activities directed toward others. It is at this point that morality loses both its Old Testament and modern utilitarian connotations. When the good is done because failure to do so entails punishment, or when goodness is measured in the context of a calculus of pain and pleasure, there is no true morality. Only when right behavior naturally emanates from a truly independent self—from an individual who is neither physically nor psychologically fixated on external conditions for self-identity—is such behavior *intrinsically* good.

This brings us to the social impact of psycho-spiritual growth. Only when the other, whether another person or another country, becomes an object of compassion and appreciation and not merely a means to a personal end, can social and international harmony prevail.

If religion is identified with some of its unfortunate consequences—imposing standards of conduct on basically unwilling subjects or misdirected idol worship (whatever that idol might be) or the systematic economic exploitation of those who can least afford it—then the true goal of "religion" is to transcend itself. Religion in its purest form is the key that unlocks the human spirit from all forms of dependence, exploitation, and subjugation. It never cultivates such dependence. Satisfaction of the psycho-spiritual need, the realization of the inchoate human imperative of a higher state of consciousness, puts man at the gate of the Promised Land. As Bucke wrote in *Cosmic Consciousness*: "In contrast with the flux of cosmic consciousness, all religions known and named today will be melted down. The soul will be revolutionized" (Bucke 1901, Introduction).

Does psycho-spiritual growth have a practical application in the modern world? Could it contribute to bringing about the "new way of thinking" Einstein saw as the only solution to the nuclear dilemma? Does such progression have practical aspects? How can man further his own psycho-spiritual destiny? The next and last chapter will outline how life in the twenty-first century will be very different from our own and how this may contribute to the widespread pursuit of self-development.

11
The Enlightened Society

To this point, I have sketched the broad outlines of an emerging world view, a paradigm for twenty-first century society. The philosophy outlined is naturalistic. Metaphysically, I have endorsed a brand of emergent evolutionism, underwritten by the notion that reality is constituted by a series of ontological levels, each of which has emerged from a prior level. In accordance with this, the social ethic proposed might be deemed "transcendent humanism," the idea, put in sophistic terms, that man is the measure of all things—but not man as he *is*. Rather, it is man *as he could be* which is the ideal to be realized and by which all others must be measured. Further, I have propounded a developmental psychology of man—developmental not only in the two distinct senses elaborated by Darwin and Piaget, but in the sense that individually man may have a hand in his own development, that he may continue to evolve in a psychospiritual sense throughout life. There is one important aspect of human development, however, which I have omitted, or perhaps *avoided*, so far. I am referring to the possibility of moral development. Put basically, what value is there in evolution if all the physical, psychological, and socioeconomic progress that has been made is not accompanied by a corresponding moral development? The question, posed most succinctly, must be: Have we, individually and as a culture, become morally better?

The Concept of Moral Evolution

One of the most controversial debates in modern academic anthropology, sociology, and history is whether there has been any significant sense in which we, as a culture, are progressing morally. The lines are drawn on the issue, with advocates of the claim of moral progress and those who reject it. Near the end of his momentous work *A History of Western Morals,* Crane Brinton takes the latter view: "We seem in sum not much better and not much worse, morally, than the Jewish and Greek founders of our moral tradition" (Brinton 1959, 445). Opponents of this view cite the abolition of slavery, the outlawing of infanticide, and the greatly improved social, political, and economic climate of the twentieth century—the era of civil rights, welfare benefits for the poor, and penal among other reforms. Proponents retort that slavery has been replaced by a social and economic subjugation of the lower classes as debilitating as forced servitude; infanticide is supplanted with abortion, a more immediate means to the same end as infanticide; further, the social and political reforms of our century are meager, sometimes disregarded by those with whom their enforcement has been entrusted. At any rate, whatever advances have been made are overshadowed by two world wars, attempted genocide, and the specter of nuclear obliteration. The case against moral progress is indeed a compelling one.

The issue is more revealing, perhaps even tragic, when cast in a different light. Whichever stand is taken on the prospect for moral progress, there is one undeniable proposition, namely, that in Western society moral progress falls far behind technological progress. Brinton notes the disparity between the two: "We have now the material possibility of destroying our civilization and, to judge by the recent record, our morals are such in practice that it seems by no means unlikely that we shall avail ourselves of this possibility" (Brinton 1959, 413).

Not too long ago, the Stanford Research Institute undertook an analysis of all of the alternative future histories, or future courses of events, that our world might see. Of all of these various possibilities, there were only two which did not end in collective disaster. The first is designated "friendly fascism" and reveals a world more or less controlled by one multinational corporation. Government would be highly centralized in a small group of business elite, who would wield the political power, ostensibly installing heads of state, manipulating the press, and pulling the economic strings. This view posits a centrally orchestrated multinational political and economic interdependence. A rigid, tenuous peace would be implemented from the top down, where social and political freedoms become functions of the ability of the state to allow them. It is in this possibility that the Orwellian republic would have come of age.

The second alternative is contingent upon a necessary "evolutionary transformation." This transformation is basically ideological and moral in nature. The shift would: "1) entail an ecological ethic, 2) place the highest value on self-development, 3) be multi-valued, multi-faceted and integrative, 4) involve the balancing and coordinating of satisfactions, rather than simply attempting to satisfy one narrowly defined field—economics, 5) convey a holistic sense of perspective or understanding to life, and 6) be experimental, open-minded, and evolutionary" (Russell, 1976).

In a very real sense, this requisite evolutionary step is a *moral* as well as an ideological shift. Moral progress, as insignificant as it may have been historically to this point, will be called upon to counteract the precarious condition in which its more successful brother has placed us. But moral progress is an altogether different entity from material or technological progress. Technological progress is an easily socialized process. Only one genius need invent the wheel for all others to benefit from it. Once originated, ideas, however prodigious, may be readily duplicated. But one man's moral progress cannot be so distributed. In the moral realm each of us must, so to speak, reinvent the wheel for ourselves. Technological genius gives us results, but moral genius leaves us with only an example. More often than not, this example is ignored, even repudiated.

The central question must now be faced. What has psychological growth, to which we have devoted the greater portion of this book, to do with moral growth? Indeed, the twentieth century has witnessed the cleavage developed between moral and psychological health. Once again, a reticent metaphysical change in view is responsible for this. Formerly, mental activity was thought largely synonymous with that of the soul. But the twentieth century, the era of the despiritualization of psychology, has come to distinguish the mind, with the attendant intellectual and emotional faculties, from the soul, with its deeper moral functions. The study of the mind was taken out of the realms of philosophy and theology and restricted to the province of science. But as any scientist will surely attest, morality is not to be studied scientifically. The *is,* but not the *ought,* may be empirically verified.

Some attempts have been made recently to bring the study of moral development into a scientific context, most notably the studies of the psychologist Lawrence Kohlberg. Kohlberg has evaluated the moral development of children, using a classification of six different levels of motivation for doing what is right or refraining from doing what is wrong. The lowest level is the threat of punishment or the promise of reward, with rationales like wanting to make a good impression at intermediate levels. The highest motive is doing good simply because it is good, and doing so neither from hope of reward nor from fear of punishment. (Kohlberg 1983)

Kohlberg's hierarchy has been questioned by critics for

a number of reasons. The most important charge is that he has imposed his own moral judgments onto the structure of the hierarchy. Still, a compelling argument in his defense is that no specific value judgments are made in the hierarchy. Instead, moral development is viewed as a progression of psychological motives. The scheme does not say *what* is right; it simply looks at the motivation for the behavior. However, attempts like Kohlberg's to bring the study of morality under the auspices of science have largely been resisted by modern psychologists.

With the compartmentalization of the mind of modern man came the de-emphasis of the moral and spiritual aspects of mind. Twentieth-century culture has witnessed the result of this process most characteristically in the advent of the "me generation." A renewed interest in inner growth was not accompanied by an acceptance of the increased moral responsibilities that come with self-development. Rather than altruism, the "culture of narcissism" exhibited the most alarming display of neurotic, self-indulgent introspectionism. The search for psychological stability is futile when one has abnegated one of the most important psychic functions—the need for self-expression in the context of morality. The beauty of psycho-spiritual evolution lies in the fact that one cannot truly develop oneself without helping others.

Moral evolution is the sine qua non of psycho-spiritual development. An understanding of this is evident in the Eastern traditions where spiritual leaders send their students out to do good deeds as a prerequisite to advanced study. One of the four paths of yoga, karma yoga, promises spiritual advancement through a life of acts of benevolence. In the Western tradition, the concept of "good works," by which the devout may secure passage to heaven, reflects this same sentiment. Perhaps even more interestingly, a number of modern psychologists have theorized that neurosis is nothing but a cycle of maladjusted thought and action. When one thinks poorly of himself, he acts in accordance with this self-image through a variety of destructive behaviors, partly out of habit and partly as a reaction to dissatisfaction with himself. This action further contributes to the unhealthy self-image. Thus, neurosis is seen as an escalating cognitive-behavioral cycle which can be broken, the view holds, only by discontinuing the negative behavior. It is a small leap from this to assuming that positive behavior may have a similar effect on the self-image and may enhance psycho-spiritual development in an affirmative way.

Though moral development is necessary to psycho-spiritual development, once the latter occurs there is a positive impact on moral development. The process between the two is reciprocal. A life lived in sympathy and activity for the needs of others may enhance self-development and, conversely, development of self tends to enhance those attributes that are taken to be moral. The ability to love, the presence of a democratic character structure, the tendency toward altruism are all "symptoms" of the healthy personality. But why is this the case? Why are genuinely *good* lives led by those who are psychologically most secure, contented, and integrated?

Modern social psychology might interject that we are embroiled in a vicious circularity here. The problem is that we are attributing "health" precisely to those personalities that exhibit the greatest number of behaviors considered socially beneficial. In short, where there is good behavior, there is a "healthy" personality. Then we turn around and, as if stating something independently true, rather than a function of our own definition, assert that healthy people tend to be morally good.

This objection, as historically significant as it has been in the social sciences, is unfounded. There are many dimensions other than the propensity to act in a socially beneficial way by which to judge the healthy personality. Maslow has given us a list of these (see Chapters Two and Five). It is an empirical fact that people who are secure in their identity, autonomous, independent, creative, who resist conformity to culture and exhibit a democratic personality structure also tend to exhibit a number of qualities considered in some general sense to be attributes of the moral personality. On the whole they are loyal friends, deeply committed in love relationships, and caring of strangers. They are compassionate, altruistic, and decidedly unself-righteous. They are deeply interested in the welfare of others. Cast in the parlance of romanticized idealistic metaphysics, it is as if the subject, having integrated itself, now seeks to order and integrate the world around itself.

I am making a concerted attempt to avoid the question of exactly what is meant by a good or moral personality. Two thousand years of debate have not even settled the fundamental question of whether an act is made "good" by its motivation or by its consequences. As there is no hope of a resolution here, let me simply defer to the traditional view. What counts most is the person's intention in acting, even if this act should accidentally bring about unfavorable results. Insofar as the "good will" usually brings the best results, there is, for the most part, no pragmatic conflict between consequentialism and formalism.

If there is a positive relationship between healthy or integrated and morally sensitive personalities, the question *why* this is so should be examined. The process of psycho-spiritual development and integration facilitates the moral growth because it fosters two conditions that are at the heart of moral development itself. The first of these is a reduced need for self-directed behavior, and the second is a heightened awareness of the other as a person not so different from oneself. Let us examine this second condition first.

The very essence of moral inequality and political oppression is the feeling (or rationalization) of disparity between subject and object, oppressor and oppressed. There must exist a sufficient difference between master and slave, for example, or else the act of enslavement cannot be rationally justified in the mind of the oppressor. If all people are devoid of significant distinguishing characteristics, the act of oppression is tantamount to enslaving one just like oneself. This is an unpalatable psychological state, unbearable to all but the most cruel or schizophrenic. To oppress is to *distinguish.* The Greeks could enslave the "barbarians" because these foreigners, being from a lesser culture, were somehow less than men. American slavery was justified on similar grounds. Racially, the negro was less than a man—three-fifths of a man if the Constitution is to be cited. Even the oppression of women was predicated on the physical and alleged intellectual disparity between men and women. The process of fighting moral inequality must center on breaking down the perceived or presumed gulf between oppressor and oppressed.

One of the most fundamental and far-reaching effects of psycho-spiritual development is the progressive obliteration of those fine lines that tend to separate people, man from woman, black from white, and even man from animal. In fact, the archetypal mystical experience, the sense of entirely transcending the subject/object dichotomy, is an extreme example of this. The result of this process is not that one overlooks differences in intelligence, physical ability, and all other attributes, but rather they simply become less important in determining how others are to be treated. One comes to regard deeper factors as more significant. For example, when the right of one living creature to slaughter another for mere sport is predicated on the difference in intelligence level, then man is justified in killing wild animals, insofar as he is more intelligent. But when the criterion becomes ability to suffer or awareness of pain, there is no distinction between man and beast. Since both feel pain equally, the ground of superiority is lost (Singer, 1981).

The very epitome of psycho-spiritual development is to look beyond accidents of nature—physical or mental handicaps, accidents of birth, social class, affluence, education, and accidents of character—in assessing moral rights. While intelligence, physical ability, or other attributes may determine certain cultural rights—who becomes a doctor and who is put in menial capacities—

moral rights must be predicated on the more essential element of our equality as self-conscious beings. Thus, even if it could be empirically established that one race was, on the whole, more intelligent than another—a dubious possibility—moral or political inequality would not be justified, because moral equality must be predicated on something more fundamental than difference in I.Q.

Stated differently, the essence of the moral sentiment is willingness to treat others as one would like to be treated oneself, with respect and appreciation. The greater similarity one sees between himself and another, the more predisposed he will be toward acting in a just way towards the other. Psycho-spiritual development fosters the sense of similarity, of community, of oneness with the other, because it causes one to focus on more essential qualities that are common to everyone—humanness, commonality as conscious beings—rather than the more superficial differences. Thus, psycho-spiritual development nurtures moral sentiment.

The other way in which moral development is enhanced by psycho-spiritual growth results from the fact that, with each progression an individual makes in the hierarchy of needs, self-integrative behavior becomes increasingly contingent on *other*-directed behavior. The lowest needs —for food, water, and shelter—are singularly self-directed. Social organization may contribute to achieving the goal of the need—hunting in groups, for example—but the need itself is not directed towards others in the community. With the need for love, however, satisfaction is completely dependent on the other and is impossible to satisfy in the absence of another. Similarly, the needs for belongingness and esteem require companionship. Self-actualization is itself contingent on participation in the greater social fabric. This accounts for Maslow's statement that every actualized person whom he studied was committed to a cause greater than himself.

With the process of self-development, an interesting shift occurs. Though the highly integrated person genuinely needs to be involved with others in a synergistic way, he needs to give rather than to take in the relationship. He becomes less the object or consumer of such interactions and increasingly the benefactor. Thus, every integrated person must take the role of boddhisattva, committed to helping those at a lesser stage than himself. In so doing, he further enhances his own development.

Despite the recent advances in modern jurisprudence in the West, manifested everywhere from the constitutional guarantees to universal suffrage to civil rights and equal education, there seems to be a disparity or lag between social and individual development. Supreme Court decisions called for the end of segregation while a majority of the people in America still supported it. Civil rights laws were hotly contested, and welfare and penal reform have always been the subject of great controversy. We are, on one hand, forced to take seriously the claims of those who see little progress on the level of the individual. On the other hand, however, we must also note the change in sentiment that has gained force in the last two decades—a sentiment that heralds the growth of that "evolutionary ethic" required in order to survive as individuals, as a culture and, perhaps, even as a planet. Now that we have excelled technologically and in providing material goods here in the West, we must countenance a new and wider meaning of the term "progress," including that of moral progress. As economist and social historian Kenneth Boulding has written:

> Now that the transition [to use science to promote a new ecological ethic and new morality] is under way, however, there is no going back on it. We must learn to use its enormous potential for good rather than for evil, and we must learn to diminish and eventually eliminate the dangers which are inherent in it (Boulding 1964, 191).

Mandate for the Enlightened Society

Having conceived a hero for our story, a goal for all mankind—the self-realized man—I am now near the end of my work. But there is a wider question to address. What of the culture that nurtures this self-integrated individual? What might it be like?

No comprehensive view of twenty-first century life, replete with predictions of economic trends, social attitudes, the state of technology, and the role of world politics, is possible here. In fact, even among the experts there is general disagreement as to the prognosis of the state of the world fifty or one hundred years from now. Views range from unbounded optimism, as characterized by Kahn's famous work *The Year 2000,* to unmitigated pessimism. The "prophets of boom" herald a world where technological innovation and political and economic prosperity inaugurate the age of plenty. Science will transcend itself by fostering the development of technology that will better what man already has and negate the instrumentalities of destruction that caused such concern a century earlier. We will learn to do more with less, conserving energy and putting industrial waste to use in cybernetic recycling plants. We will have discovered methods for eliminating pollution, controlling the population, increasing the average life span and, in general, promoting economic, political, and social welfare and harmony. This is twenty-first century society at its best.

There is another school of thought, however, diametrically opposed to this rosy view. The so-called "prophets of doom" project a world of material depletion and psychological exhaustion. Even if we do not destroy ourselves with nuclear weapons, we will "die with a whimper" rather than a bang. The neo-Malthusian argues that overpopulation, the shortage of resources and energy, as well as corruption of the ecological balance of the planet portend only the most horrible of existences for those only a generation or two away.

On both sides, while some proponents are extreme, there are many futurists at intermediate positions as well (Cornish 1977). Whatever position is taken, however, one thing seems agreed by all: that man is now at a major crossroads, not only in the history of civilization, but with respect to his own evolution. We can determine the future course that the world is to take, but to do so we must have an idea of our own purpose in the world. As biologist Julian Huxley wrote several decades ago:

> The future of man, if it is to be progress and not merely a standstill or a degeneration, must be guided by a deliberate purpose. . . . Progress is a major fact of past evolution; but it is limited to a few select stocks. It may continue in the future, but it is not inevitable; man, by now become the trustee of evolution, must work and plan if he is to achieve further progress for himself and for life (Harmon 1981).

Every society in the past has had some overarching goal that indued daily existence with a meaning. This goal was built into the very social institutions that constituted culture, and was thus passed from generation to generation, induing the constituents of each society with a sense of history. It seems we have now transcended these traditional goals. They have served their purpose, but now we must move on. We must understand the human condition as dynamic, not static, evolutionary rather than preordained and fixed.

What are the goals of the enlightened society? They are twofold. First, as a culture that has largely fulfilled the material needs of its constituents, we must mandate a new and higher goal: the psycho-spiritual, rather than simply material, development of man. We must create new institutions and reformulate older institutions fashioned for developing the total individual.

The second goal of the enlightened society will be the promotion of economic, technological, and sociopolitical progress for the poor in the world. This includes both those in the Third World and at home, in developed and underdeveloped nations alike. Because the enlightened society cannot exist meaningfully in an unenlightened world, the other great goal of the West must be to contribute to sufficiently raising the standard of living in the Third World—literally two-thirds of the global population—so as to create a Having base on which further development may be built. Bereft of this improvement, worldwide political and economic discord will ultimately affect even a healthy society in isolation. Further, the increasing political and economic interdependence among nations will serve only to intensify this in the future. Thus, international economic amelioration is as essential to the self-interest of the progressive minority as it is to the lagging masses.

The enlightened society must deal with these imperatives in novel and innovative ways, effectively reshaping the character of culture as we will know it. The reorganization, with its major emphasis on psycho-spiritual development, will reorder traditional social concepts and institutions, completely transforming the fabric of everyday existence. Let me paint in broad strokes some of the changes that might be expected.

In the realm of work, perhaps the most important force in contemporary culture, a new motivation must evolve. There surely will be less available work in the years to come, a result of increasing technological efficiency which will automate many of the tasks formerly performed by human labor. Some have predicted that the rise of service industries will provide jobs which were lost in areas of production and which can be performed more effectively with machines. But it seems unlikely that this will absorb the large numbers of people traditionally employed in areas of production. Further, as the locus of employment comes to shift increasingly to the Third World, a trend already powerfully in operation today, there will be a shortage of traditional forms of work in the developed nations, though the standard of living may continue to rise. In this situation, there will be less economic need for work, though there will still be the psychological need for work as a means to a sense of individual worth and self-fulfillment. What will become of work? Willis Harman, social researcher and futurist, prescribes the following:

> The required new thinking can be simply stated. In a technologically advanced society where production of

> sufficient goods and services can be handled with ease, *employment exists for self-development and is only secondarily concerned with the production of goods and services* (emphasis in the original). (Harmon 1981, 178)

In the years ahead, society will be forced to develop more equitable distribution of employment. Indeed, employment will become something of a commodity, as creative, meaningful work will be increasingly sought. Rather than allowing some of the population to be employed while a significant proportion are cyclically or chronically unemployed, the work week will be shortened per individual as employment is distributed among more people.

The increasing amount of free time envisioned by this prognosis will mean that new activities will come to fill this time. Self-development—physical, intellectual, and psycho-spiritual—will be important as people will be able to devote greater portions of their lives to bettering themselves as human beings. Traditional education, as well as old and new forms of self-integrative activities, will become more prevalent. As meditation, biofeedback, and newly developed forms of self-development become popular, leisure will take on less the function of tension release, as facilitated by various forms of socially and personally destructive behavior, and will become a means to self-expression and development.

Education in the enlightened society is a particularly important and fascinating subject. Education of the individual must come to mean something more than it now does. It must foster and enhance self-development at every level, from grade school to adult education programs. The traditional disparity between intelligence and wisdom must be overcome in the twenty-first century scholar. Both qualities should be embodied in the future educator. Today, stories abound of the most creative and intelligent people who also happen to be cold, impersonal, arrogant, or even self-destructive. A recent psychological study has shown that people characteristically associate meanness of temperament with intelligence: where all other factors were equal, the more arrogant or unkind individual was perceived to be more intellectually gifted. A related version of this social myth is the belief that the most creative are often the most unstable or self-destructive. The lives of many of the greatest poets, writers, and artists may be more a result of this prevailing mythology than proof of its validity. Modern education must obliterate these myths by the example of the future scholar and by teaching *self*-development along with the mastery of an intellectual discipline. Future teachers should carry the example of self-development, psycho-spiritually as well as intellectually, to the highest level of all. They should be the most shining examples of humanity, in the fullest sense of the word.

Education of the future should be the purveyor of the ethic of self-development, the notion of self-integration as an on-going process being made central. Further, schools should convey the various means to accomplish this goal, and there should be a progressive development of techniques through the various grades of education to achieve this end. Finally, future education should make strides in the direction of debalkanization and reintegration of the various academic disciplines. Today very little communication between different university departments fosters the notion that each respective field has little of relevance to any other field. On the contrary, philosophy and law, medicine and the humanities, business and communication studies, "hard" science and social science all have much to offer one another. The connections between various academic disciplines must become known. Ultimately, the reversal of psychological fragmentation must be accompanied by a parallel process at the institutional level. Education is the most obvious and effective place to begin.

Science must also play a renewed and revitalizing role in the enlightened society. Particularly in the human sciences, the serious study of physiological and psychological changes in the individual, resulting from meditation, biofeedback, and other technologies of self-development, must take place. Science must also take part in discovering new and more powerful means of self-integration. This process has begun with the work in biofeedback, which has already been used to control everything from heartbeat to ovulation to the release of endomorphines to kill pain. With the aid of this and other similar technologies, man of the future may increasingly bring what were previously thought to be involuntary or automatic bodily processes under mental control. In this manner, we may begin to eliminate the need for drugs or other artificial medical practices, extending the reach of the conscious mind to the entire organism (Morgan 1980, 113).

Science will also increasingly explore sleep and the process of dreaming, to gain new insights into the operation of the brain. It may be possible to stimulate REM sleep, the deepest level of sleep where dreaming occurs. In humans REM sleep, which may be the only beneficial period of sleep, occurs only a third of the normal sleeping period. By facilitating solid REM sleep, science may be able to cut the necessary sleep time down to two or three hours a night. These and other similar prospects clearly demonstrate that twenty-first century life will be as fascinating as it is different from contemporary existence. Science will be a significant force in this process.

Before science can take its place in the role here forecast, a change in philosophical perspective, particularly with respect to the human sciences, is required. Specifically, psychology will have to forsake its current methodological commitment to experimentation in a manner similar to a hard science. Human consciousness must come to be recognized as an entity independent of external behavior or neural activity. The significance of internal psychological states must be acknowledged as a legitimate object of study, though, of course, new "non-objective" methods for this study must be developed. It is important that practitioners in the human sciences realize that each discipline may have its own epistemology and methodology. Psychology need not ape physics as having the only viable framework for scientific research.

Religion in the enlightened society must also play a renewed role in the fabric of daily existence and in the individual's search for self-realization. But religion will come to have a new meaning, a solid significance to the common man, which it has largely lost in our time. Not in doctrine or dogma, but in experience will future man realize the true nature of spirituality. To be sure, the traditional religions will not die out in the next century. Instead, traditional doctrine may be increasingly discarded, as is already patently obvious in modern Judaism, Catholicism, and the Protestant religions. Narrowly defined myths will give way to the universalist concept of self-realization. A reinterpretation of the traditional religions may occur, reassessing the central goal of each to be evolution and enlightenment. The message of the great prophets from the Buddha to the Christ and beyond will be reviewed and recast in terms of self-actualization, a common thread among all the world's religions thus being made possible. For many, the current prevailing notion that self-development is selfish, or worse, a repudiation of God, will be viewed as was the ancient admonition against modern medicine as an obstruction of God's will.

Religion in the enlightened society will come to have a very personal tone, and will be intimately bound up with philosophy, psychology, and the life sciences. The traditional antipathy between sciences and religion will be overcome as the old myths, in both science and religion, are exploded. Further, there will be a new intimacy between religion and morality, as morality comes to be seen as a function of psycho-spiritual development, which is also the object of the religious imperative.

Other developments may further the religious aspects of spiritual development. The next century may witness the rise of a class of secular priests, a group of intellectually and spiritually perfected men and women devoted to preserving and developing the knowledge of self-integration and to helping others in this. This group might be composed of lawyers, philosophers, and writers committed to social and political as well as spiritual development. This group might be modelled after the Jewish Pharisees, the wisest and most learned of the Jews, who were inaccurately portrayed in the New Testament as sophists and traitors (Maccoby 1986).

Renewed interest in spiritual goals would also have an impact on the reintegration of the family and in promoting the traditional values of love, fraternity, and community. An antidote to the trend toward transience and fragmentation, the important traditional aspects of life may be preserved. At the same time, this revitalized interest in self-development should never be taken to herald the advent of otherworldly asceticism or puritan anti-sensualism. This picture of the future should portend a loving, joyful, and *natural* existence, filled with the pleasures that we, as human beings, are capable of enjoying. Life should be long, full of friendship and love, and it should be deeply experienced.

The enlightened society is a place where diversity and cooperation thrive together, where the world at large, with all its constituent forms, will be made sacred. That which is profane is simply that which is set apart from the process of the evolution of consciousness. But all that lives is part of this process. The citizens of the enlightened society will have cultivated the knowledge of this in themselves. They will have passed the stage of meaninglessness and transcended the search for self-identity, having found their identity in progressive self-development.

The enlightened society is the place where all share a common goal, though they will have found a diversity of paths in reaching this goal. It is not a place where each person recklessly pursues his own interests at the expense of others. Rather, the common good will be served simultaneously by all who pursue that good by developing themselves into better human beings. It is a culture, unlike any before, where personal interaction has reached a more genuine, open, and compassionate level. The isolation and alienation, the loneliness and despair will be left behind, symptoms of a lesser civilization. In the fullest sense, the narcissistic culture will have become the enlightened society.

In the end, modern man must recognize that the human species has already made whatever evolutionary progress that is possible by waging war on external nature. The modern Prometheus must look inward to discover the greatest secrets of the universe, as well as the greatest rewards. He will bring the fire of the gods to his own consciousness. It is not space but mind that constitutes the final frontier. Once man has developed to his fullest potential, the rest of the universe can pose no insurmountable problem. Once man has conquered himself, he will have conquered all.

These are the mandates of the enlightened society.

Appendix

The Problem of Mind in the Material World

The problem of the relationship between mind and body is perhaps the most fundamental philosophical problem confronting humankind. The pages that follow present an investigation of some of the traditional problems, issues, and answers given to this problem. This discussion clears the way for a naturalistic view of man that allows for enlightenment as a factor in evolution, the view put forth in this book.

The Concept of Mind

The twentieth century has witnessed a strange turn of events with respect to the materialism-dualism controversy. Those opposed to the materialistic program have historically rebuffed the materialistic attacks by simply asserting that living creatures, though they may be partially material beings, act in ways that inert matter does not. Living creatures move, grow, and, more significantly, reproduce. There is some *extra* component added to matter that serves to animate it. Thus the concept of soul took its place as the captain of the physical ship. (It is interesting to note that this same argument was often not extended to the animal kingdom. Though lower order species were also obviously animate, religious dogma often denied them a soul, thus leaving them in a limbo between the inanimate and soul-bearing man. This contention effectively contradicts the dualist's own argument that soul is a necessary component of the living.)

The ever-burgeoning power of science forced the dualist to retrace his steps and take a position slightly different from that traditionally espoused. With the artificial synthesis of urea in 1828, the previous position that nothing organic could come from the inorganic had to be relinquished. The major modern advance of this order took place in 1953 when Stanley Miller produced amino acids, the basic building blocks of protein and ultimately life, by passing electric current (analogous to lightning) through a mixture of ammonia, nitrogen, and other elements (representative of the atmosphere of primeval earth). With such advances, the soul-component theory became improbable.

In retreat the dualist took the high ground. It was not *life* that represented the fundamental barrier to materialism, but *Mind.* And though the materialist laid siege to this final fortress, the slings and arrows of science could not touch Mind. Though the material brain processes could be pointed to as the physical component in the mental, materialists could not easily deny an immaterial mental realm consisting of nonphysical thoughts, desires, intentions or, in short, awareness.

The issue is actually more subtle than it at first appears. This is because there are two different dualist positions. The first, what we shall call "supernatural dualism," posits the existence of a mental substance which is completely independent of the physical. This view holds that mind and matter are two completely distinct irreducible substances and "never the twain shall meet." This strange substance is sometimes held to exist independently of any living creature, to serve as an underlying organizing force in nature that goes by a number of different names: Mind, Overmind, or Consciousness. This view, actually a group of similar theories, makes two broad claims. First, the mental is that which cannot be translated, converted, or reduced to physical terms. The thinking of a thought is a fundamentally different kind of thing from a material object. The former is private, does not seem to have a spatial location, and is often described as easily in action or verb terms as it is in object terms. (For example, I *think* a thought, or I *desire* something.) On the other hand, matter is publicly observable, exists in space and time, and is described in noun-terms, as a substance or passive object.

The second claim of supernatural dualism is more radical. It holds that Mind is not only basically different from matter; it is actually independent of matter in that, though mind and matter may act on and interact with one another, the destruction of the material does not entail the dissolution of Mind. This notion is, of course, nothing other than an updated version of the Platonic-Christian soul.

The second type of dualism, what I shall call "ontological dualism," is less "metaphysical" and asserts only the first of the two claims. Ontological dualism holds that the mental is something radically different from, and irreducible to, the physical, but it is still *causally dependent* on material events for its existence. Thus the death of the body precipitates a crumbling of the mental house of cards.

Surprisingly, many modern materialists argue against this version of dualism as feverishly as the first, because ontological dualism seems to represent a symbolic threat to the reductionist unity of materialism. It seems that such philosophers equate the rejection of materialism with an affirmative answer to the most personal of all metaphysical questions: Can conscious experience exist independently of the body? Further, even though the mental is completely dependent on the physical for its continued existence, its ontological disparity from the physical places the materialist in the position of having to admit that there are things in the universe that are not "things" in the usual sense. To the dyed-in-the-wool materialist, this is as repugnant a notion as the concept of an immortal soul.

An examination of some of the major materialistic theories of mind follows. The rejection of these will leave the door open for ontological dualism and the possibility that mind may not only affect matter, but can sometimes bring about an outright reorganization of the material world.

Problems of Mind in the Material World

There are basically three sets of insurmountable problems that confront any attempt to answer the mind-body problem. First, there is the problem of causal connection. Basically, common sense tells us that we think a thought or decide to take some action, say to lift the right arm, and then the physical action follows. The thought is believed to be nonphysical—it does not occur anywhere in space. How could a nonspatial, nonphysical intention cause a physical action? All of our current scientific laws cover only those processes that occur in space and time; in other words, that act on the physical plane. Scientists and philosophers are in the position of having two options: either accepting that there are transphysical laws and processes, in other words processes that occur on levels of reality which cannot be properly called "matter" or "energy," or proposing that mind does not affect matter. Preferring to relinquish mind rather than to accept that there is much more to reality than currently understood, scientists have traditionally rejected the former option in favor of the latter. This alleged interaction between nonphysical volition and physical movement, then, is the problem of the causal connection between matter and mind.

The second barrier to solving the mind-body problem particularly for the materialistic paradigm is the problem of reductionism. In order to disprove dualism, the materialist must demonstrate that such things as thoughts, ideas, desires, and feelings either do not exist or can be explained in material terms. Further, "explain" does not simply mean that the materialist must demonstrate a causal connection or isomorphism between brain process and idea; he must be able to describe the *thought itself* as either a material thing or a property of the physical. This is not as easy as it may at first appear. As noted earlier, thoughts and feelings seem to have fundamentally different types of existences from that of the material world. Thoughts are private and knowable only to the subject. They are nonspatial. Matter, on the other hand, is publicly accessible, spatially situated, and exists in a passive, nonactive sense. Seen from a different standpoint, thought cannot be simply brain processes because where a subject may have a thought of red, he does not have a red brain process (Smart 1981, 160). Further, the brain process may involve certain physical activities—the firing of neurons, the swerve of particles—that in no way are reflected in the resultant thought. The problem, then, stems from the fact that we cannot reduce mental predicates to material properties or terms.

Finally, the third set of problems surrounding the nature of mind, and confronting all theorists of mind equally, materialist or otherwise, is the problem of intentionality. Franz Brentano set the mental apart from the material by asserting that only mental events have other things outside themselves as objects (Aquila, 1977). Matter is inert and unaware of anything, itself or the world around it. But states of mind are those that take for their object other states of matter and/or mind. In fact, the mental is the only thing that divides itself into subject and object. But this leads to a host of paradoxes. First, if there is a subject and an object, where exactly does consciousness fit in? Is it, on one hand, that which *relates* subject and object, acting as a medium between the two? Or is consciousness coextensive with the subject itself? (James 1918, 199). And what exactly is the subject anyway? One can never know the subject as subject. The introspector can examine his thoughts, patterns of thoughts, and even underlying personal motives for a given thought pattern, but whenever the subject attempts to look at itself, it can only call up these entities as objects. Yet there is always something *else* that is doing the introspection. The subject lies forever just beneath the surface, always grasping, never grasped. It seems to accompany every thought, but is not the thought itself.

The problems of causal connection between body and mind, the ontological reduction of the mental to the physical, and the paradox of subject and object are the three enigmas of the mind-body problem. Let us now examine actual proposed solutions to the mind-body problem, materialist and otherwise.

Interactionism

Every man, and this includes philosophers in their less perverse moments, subscribes to the notion of *interactionism.* This is the idea that mind and body are separate and distinct, and that each may act on the other. This theory seems to fail fundamentally because it cannot answer the problem of causal connection: How do the material and nonmaterial influence one another? How does a thought bring about a brain process?

Secondly, there does not seem to be any mental independence in that science has learned to affect almost any mental change by means of a physical cause (Snyder 1975, 10-38). Science has shown that it is now possible to change the mood, amount of tension, alertness, clarity of mind, coordination, and even introduce or destroy certain memory patterns in an organism. Memory transfer from animal to animal has been achieved in experiments where one laboratory rat, for example, is taught a specific and complex task. Portions of the brain of this first animal were subsequently transferred to a second rat, which then performed the complex activity. Thus thought-transfer by physical means seems imminently possible. With this in mind, what role is left for the passive thought? This framework leaves the mental with no other function than that of an impotent side-effect to signal the physical transition. Thoughts seem merely to reflect changes in brain chemistry.

Epiphenomenalism

This takes us to the second of this group of theories—epiphenomenalism. This is the view of man as conscious automata. By this theory, the existence of a mental realm is granted, but is held to be completely subordinate to, and dependent upon, the physical brain process. William James likened the function of consciousness in this view to that of the shadow. It follows wherever the body goes but has no reciprocal effect.

T.H. Huxley reports the contention as follows:

> It seems to me that in men, as in brutes, there is no proof that any state of consciousness is the cause of change in the motion of the matter of the organism. If these positions are well based, it follows that our mental conditions are simply the symbols in consciousness of the change which takes place automatically in the organism; and that to take an extreme illustration, the feeling we call volition is not the cause of a voluntary act, but a symbol of that state of the brain which is the immediate cause of that act. We are conscious automata (quoted in James 1918, 131).

This theory, then, is different from extreme materialism in that it acknowledges the existence of the mental and the disparity between the two realms. It thus avoids the problem of ontological reductionism. But the theory is insufficient on some counts and simply wrong on still others.

The first problem is perhaps at most an aesthetic problem, but is problematic nonetheless. Why did consciousness evolve if it was to have no function? Spinoza once said that if a rock flying through the air was suddenly to become conscious, it would think that it was willing its flight and subsequent fall. We, as conscious beings, are in exactly this state, according to the epiphenomenalist.

As William James pointed out, however, everything that has developed as a result of evolution has had a particular function. What would be the evolutionary status of this superfluous epiphenomenon we call conscious activity? Secondly, what exactly is this mental activity, and how does the physical *cause* it?

Another problem arises as the result of the implied isomorphism between brain process and mental event. There are, no doubt, many processes occurring in the brain at any given time. Some of these will be correlated with the given mental event, while others will go "unnoticed." For example, there may be an indefinite number of neural processes occurring simultaneously, but we are aware of only one at a time. What is making the switch in consciousness between the different processes? Why are we conscious of only one of them?

Finally, perhaps the most insurmountable problem comes to us from the realm of common sense, a territory too seldom canvassed by the conjecturer. C.D. Broad uses an example which will be instructive: Suppose there is a very morally upstanding man, a teacher, who is spending a great deal of extra time with a particular female student. He does so because he believes he is helping the student and because he believes she needs his help. But a truer rendering of motive shows him to be helping the girl because he is attracted to her, and in fact, desires her. He goes on spending the extra time with the student until a friend brings it to his attention that he may desire the student sexually. Upon becoming aware of his true motive, he changes his behavior and greatly reduces the time spent with the student. If this account is at all realistic, which it seems to be, then the *awareness* of the young teacher's true motive caused a change in behavior. Epiphenomenalism must then be rejected (Broad, 1925).

Behaviorism

Another major theory that has flourished in the twentieth century is behaviorism. Originally propounded by John Watson in the late nineteenth century and later popularized by B.F. Skinner, behaviorism is more accurately characterized as an offshoot of the postivistic (methodological) tradition than the materialist (metaphysical) notion. There seems to be some controversy among behaviorists as to the status of the mental, whether it is nonexistent or simply unimportant. Basically, this theory follows the notion of epiphenomenalism. Thoughts, feelings, desires, hopes, and other mental currency can never be studied objectively. Therefore, they are unimportant aspects of the person's behavior. The behaviorist thus deals with mind by rejecting or ignoring it. All that need to be accounted for are the modes of outward behavior, along with the corresponding role of stimulus and mode of conditioning.

While there are many interesting implications of this view, we shall examine only the most modern and sophisticated version of behaviorism. Where behaviorism in its crude form asserts that having a pain is nothing more than wincing, crying out, or other behaviors that commonly accompany pain, the more sophisticated version attempts to contend with feeling itself in behavioristic terms.

B.A. Farrell combines a dispositional analysis of behavior with the notion that feeling is a sort of "covert" behavior. He points out that psychology (at least behaviorism) does not include the study of the sensation or felt quality of, say, a rat discriminating a red disc, or our thoughts and emotional states that accompany our disposition to act in a certain way. Farrell goes on to assert that the "raw feels" themselves are a covert type of behavior. This is a significant philosophical move, precisely because behaviorists previously were in the position of ascribing everything to behavioral explanation—everything, that is, except for feeling itself. For example, in the seminal work *The Concept of Mind,* Gilbert Ryle attempts to show that all beliefs, desires, and other mental coinage are simply dispositions to behave in a certain way. As an instance of this, a given subject *believes* the world is round just in case he is willing to put the belief to the test, to sail around the world, for example. Belief is simply a disposition to act. Likewise a desire for food is nothing more than a disposition to seek out a meal and eat. But Ryle had to stop short of the feeling itself. He was not able to analyze away the subjective *feeling* of being hungry in behavioristic terms. Pain gives dispositional behaviorists a particular problem. There simply is more to pain than the cry, the retracting of the hand, and the subsequent avoidance of the hot oven. There is a felt aspect.

It is precisely this aspect that Farrell attempts to analyze in terms of "covert" behavior. But it seems clear that this phrase is simply a subterfuge for an issue that will not be assailed in behavioristic terms. Behaviorism fails on all three counts outlined above. It does not tell us what the "felt aspect" is; it fails to explain the causal role of subjective mental states; and it does not provide us with an understanding of subjective experience of the subject-object dichotomy.

There is also a more fundamental problem with the behaviorist's dispositional analysis of behavior. For example, when we say that a man's belief that something is poison is nothing but a disposition for him to act in a certain way, we speak as if there is *one* behavior towards which the man is disposed. And we would expect this. A disposition is a limiting type of relation—it correlates one belief with one type of action. But the behavior that will eventuate, given the man's belief that this is poison, will vary according to other factors in the situation. For example, if the man were out to catch a rat, he would bait a trap with the poison. If he found the poison near a child's play area, he would dispose of it. If he wanted to die, he would eat it himself. Thus, for the one belief that this is poison, we find perhaps an infinite number of possible behaviors toward which the man is disposed. A disposition that could lead to an infinite number of possible actions is no disposition. If belief is nothing but a disposition to act in a certain way, we are no closer to the answer of what this belief *is*. Behaviorism must thus be rejected (Campbell 1980, 65-74).

The Identity Theory

The last theory to be examined here is perhaps the most modern of the solutions to the mind-body problem. It is the identity thesis, so-called because the theory holds that consciousness *is* a brain process. This is a sophisticated version of the materialistic, reductionist scheme. J.J.C. Smart sets the picture as follows:

> It seems to me that science is increasingly giving us a viewpoint whereby organisms are able to be seen as physicochemical mechanisms: it seems that even the behavior of man himself will one day be explicable in mechanistic terms. There does seem to be, so far as science is concerned, nothing in the world but increasingly complex arrangements of physical constituents. All except for one place: in consciousness (Smart 1981, 161).

It is precisely for this reason that Smart, U.T. Place, and others have put forward the identity thesis. The theory runs as follows: Consciousness is to the brain process as lightning is to electrical disturbances in the atmosphere. They are two different meanings for the same thing. Put slightly differently, consciousness and brain process are logically or semantically distinct but ontologically one.

Smart correctly points out that a mere isomorphism or one-to-one correspondence between brain process and mental event (as in epiphenomenalism) will not do because this would demand that we countenance another type of reality beyond the physical in the cosmos. Admission of a distinct (though dependent) mental reality would be tantamount to admitting that there is something *more* to reality, something ineffable or untouchable by science.

As attractive as the identity thesis may seem to the prospective reductionist, there are fundamental problems with the theory. First of all, it appears to be only contingently true that the mental state "I am hungry" is correlative with a physical brain process. It may turn out that our current physiological theory is inaccurate, that when a subject reports a mental event, he is not reporting a brain process. Or it might be that a brain process is a necessary condition for a mental event, but is not sufficient. There are many brain processes that occur at a neural level at any given time. But there is not an attendant consciousness for each one.

Another difficulty with this view is that no one has been able to reduce qualitative mental properties—e.g. the feeling of pain—to material properties. It is simply not the case that we can reduce mental events to physical causes. Smart admits this and, in fact, concedes that there may be "psychic properties." This is tantamount to admitting that the mental is in some sense ontologically distinct, since no physical thing can have a nonphysical property.

In the end, all the reductionist theories fail. No theory, however clever, can purport to show that either mental events can be reduced to physical states, or that consciousness can have no causal import. The reductionistic paradigm, as historically understood, has never successfully met these and other challenges. Further, enough new scientific evidence exists to demonstrate that mind can have as great an effect on the body as was previously thought possible only in the direction of body to mind. Research with biofeedback, meditation, and other various techniques currently attests to the possibility of mental control over even supposedly "automatic" bodily processes. In short, mind is making its way back into science and philosophy.

Bibliography

Ajaya, Swami. 1978. Living with the Himalayan masters. Honesdale, PA: International Institute for Yoga Science and Philosophy.

Allport, Gordon W. 1950. The individual and his religion. New York: Macmillan.

Aquila, Richard E. 1977. Intentionality: a study of mental acts. University Park: Pennsylvania State University Press.

Armstrong, D.M. 1980. The nature of mind. Brighton-Sussex, England: The Harvester Press.

Ballentine, Rudolph M. 1976. "Yoga and psychoanalysis" in Psychology east and west. Edited by Swami Ajaya. Honesdale, PA: International Institute for Yoga Science and Philosophy.

Bardis, Panos D. 1981. A history of thanatology. New York: University Press of America.

Becker, Ernest. 1973. The denial of death. New York: The Free Press.

Behanan, Kovoor T. 1937. Yoga: a scientific evaluation. New York: Macmillan.

Boulding, Kenneth. 1964. The meaning of the twentieth century. New York: Harper and Row.

Brinton, Clarence Crane. 1959. A history of western morals. New York: Harcourt, Brace and Company.

Broad, C.D. 1925. The mind and its place in nature. London: Routledge and Kegan Paul Ltd.

Bucke, Richard M. 1901. Cosmic consciousness. New York: E.P. Dutton and Company.

Campbell, Anthony. 1974. Seven states of consciousness. New York: Harper and Row.

Campbell, Keith. 1980. Body and mind. Notre Dame, IN: University of Notre Dame Press.

Camus, Albert. 1955. The myth of Sisyphus. Translated by Justin O'Brien. New York: Vintage Books.

Cantril, Hadley. 1963. The psychology of social movements. New York: John Wiley and Sons.

Clark, Ronald D. 1976. The life of Bertrand Russell. New York: Alfred A. Knopf Inc.

Clark, Walter Houston. 1977. "The psychology of religious experience" in Current perspectives in the psychology of religion. Edited by H. Newton Maloney. Grand Rapids, MI: B. Eerdman's Publishing Company.

Cornish, Edward. 1979. The study of the future. Washington: World Future Society.

Farrell, B.A. 1981. "Experience," in Philosophy of mind. Edited by V.C. Chappell. New York: Dover Publications Inc.

Fort, Joel. 1981. The addicted society; pleasure seeking and punishment revisited. New York: The Grove Press.

Forum, Jack. 1973. Transcendental meditation. New York: E.P. Dutton and Company.

Fromm, Erich. 1955. The sane society. New York: Rinehart and Company.

Freud, Sigmund. 1962. Civilization and its discontents. Translated and edited by James Strachey. New York: W.W. Norton.

Hall, Calvin S. and Gardner, Lindsay. 1957. Theories of personality. New York: John Wiley and Sons.

Harmon, Willis. 1981. "Work," in Millennium: glimpses into the 21st century. Edited by Alberto Villoldo et al. Los Angeles: J.P. Tarcher.

Hoffer, Eric. 1976. In our time. New York: Morrow Quill.

Hunt, Richard A. and King, Marton B. 1977. "The intrinsic-extrinsic concept: a review and evaluation" in Current perspectives in the psychology of religion. Edited by H. Newton Maloney. Grand Rapids, MI: B. Eerdman's Publishing Company.

James, William. 1918. The principles of psychology. New York: Dover Publications.

James, William. 1961. The varieties of religious experience. New York: Collier Books.

Jourard, Sidney M. 1971. The transcendent self. New York: D. Van Nostrand Company.

Jung, C.G. 1960. On the nature of the psyche. Translated by R.F.C. Hull. Princeton, NJ: Princeton University Press.

Kohlberg, Lawrence. 1983. The psychology of moral development. Harper and Row.

Kohler, Wolfgang. 1959. "The mind-body problem" in Dimensions of mind. Edited by Sidney Hook. New York: New York University Press.

Kuhn, Thomas. 1964. The structure of scientific revolution. Chicago: University of Chicago Press.

Laing, R.D. 1967. The politics of experience. New York: Pantheon Books.

Lasch, Christopher. 1979. The culture of narcissism. New York: Warner Books.

LeShan, Lawrence. 1974. How to meditate. New York: Harper and Row.

Lifton, Robert J. 1970. "Protean man" in Relevants. Edited by Edward Quinn and Paul J. Dolan. New York: The Free Press.

Lukacs, John. 1970. The passing of the modern age. New York: Harper and Row.

Maccoby, Hyam. 1986. The mythmaker: Paul and the invention of Christianity. New York: Harper and Row.

Maslow, Abraham H. 1971. The farther reaches of human nature. New York: The Viking Press.

Maslow, Abraham H. 1964. Religions, values and peak experiences. Columbus, OH: Ohio State University Press.

Maslow, Abraham H. 1962. Toward a psychology of being. Princeton, NJ: Van Nostrand.

Merrell-Wolff, Franklin. 1973. The philosophy of consciousness without an object. New York: Crown Publishing Company.

Mitchell, Arnold. 1983. The nine American lifestyles. New York: Warner Books.

Morgan, Chris. 1980. Future man. New York: Irvington Publications.

Newman, John Cardinal. 1970. "The ideas of a university" in Relevants. Edited by Edward Quinn and Paul J. Dolan. New York: The Free Press.

Oates, Wayne Edward. 1957. The religious dimensions of personality. New York: Association Press.

Ouspensky, P.D. 1973. The psychology of man's possible evolution. New York: Vintage Books.

Pagels, Heinz R. 1982. The cosmic code. New York: Bantam Books.

Phenix, Philip H. 1964. Realms of meaning: a philosophy of the curriculum for general education. New York: McGraw Hill.

Plato. 1956. Great dialogues of Plato. Translated by W.H.D. Rouse. New York: New American Library.

Rifkin, Jeremy. 1983. Algeny. New York: Viking Press.

Roy, M.N. 1950. Fragments from a prisoner's diary: India's message. Calcutta: Renaissance Publishing Company, Ltd.

Russell, Bertrand. 1958. The will to doubt. New York: The Wisdom Press.

Russell, Peter. 1976. The TM technique. Boston: Routledge and Kegan Paul Ltd.

Singer, Peter. 1981. "All animals are equal," in Morality and moral controversies. Edited by John Arthus. Englewood Cliffs, NJ: Prentice Hall.

Smart, J.J.C. 1981. "Sensations and brain processes," in Philosophy of mind. Edited by V.C. Chappell. New York: Dover Publications Inc.

Smith, Huston. 1982. Beyond the post-modern mind. Wheaton, IL: The Theosophical Publishing House.

Smith, Huston. 1958. The religions of man. New York: Harper and Row.

Spellman, Glenn, Baskett, D., and Byrne, Don. 1977. "Manifest anxiety as a contributing factor in religious conversion" in Current perspectives in the psychology of religion. Edited by H. Newton Maloney. Grand Rapids, MI: B. Eerdman's Publishing Company.

Sperry, Roger. 1983. Science and moral priority. New York: Columbia University Press.

Stace, W.T. 1960. Mysticism and philosophy. New York: J.P. Lippincott Company.

Tart, Charles. 1980. "States of consciousness and state specific sciences," in Beyond ego: transpersonal dimensions in psychology. Edited by Roger Walsh and Francis Vaughan. Los Angeles: J.P. Tarcher Books.

Taylor, Richard. 1963. Metaphysics. Englewood Cliffs, NJ: Prentice Hall.

Toffler, Alvin. 1970. Future shock. New York: Bantam Books.

Vaughan, Frances E. 1983. "Perception and knowledge: reflections on psychological and spiritual learning in the psychedelic experience," in Psychedelic reflections. Edited by Lester Grinspoon and James B. Bakalar. New York: Human Science Press.

Walsh, Roger. 1983. "Psychedelics and self-actualization" in Psychedelic reflections. Edited by Lester Grinspoon and James B. Bakalar. New York: Human Science Press.

Index

QUEST BOOKS

are published by
The Theosophical Society in America,
a branch of a world organization
dedicated to the promotion of brotherhood and
the encouragement of the study of religion,
philosophy, and science, to the end that man may
better understand himself and his place in
the universe. The Society stands for complete
freedom of individual search and belief.
In the Theosophical Classics Series
well-known occult works are made
available in popular editions.